Robert Grosseteste, Richard Francis Weymouth

Castel off loue (Chasteau d'amour or carmen de creatione mundi)

An early English Translation of an old French Poem

Robert Grosseteste, Richard Francis Weymouth

Castel off loue (Chasteau d'amour or carmen de creatione mundi)
An early English Translation of an old French Poem

ISBN/EAN: 9783742807106

Manufactured in Europe, USA, Canada, Australia, Japa

Cover: Foto ©Andreas Hilbeck / pixelio.de

Manufactured and distributed by brebook publishing software (www.brebook.com)

Robert Grosseteste, Richard Francis Weymouth

Castel off loue (Chasteau d'amour or carmen de creatione mundi)

CASTEL OFF LOUE

(CHASTEAU D'AMOUR

OR

CARMEN DE CREATIONE MUNDI)

AN EARLY ENGLISH TRANSLATION OF AN OLD FRENCH POEM

BY

ROBERT GROSSETESTE
BISHOP OF LINCOLN.

COPIED AND EDITED FROM MSS. IN THE BRITISH MUSEUM, AND IN THE
BODLEIAN LIBRARY, OXFORD,

WITH

NOTES, CRITICAL AND EXEGETICAL, AND GLOSSARY,

BY

RICHARD FRANCIS WEYMOUTH, M.A. LOND.,
MEMBER OF THE PHILOLOGICAL SOCIETY.

ASHER & CO.,
PUBLISHERS TO THE PHILOLOGICAL SOCIETY.
LONDON: 13 BEDFORD ST., COVENT GARDEN.
BERLIN: UNTER DEN LINDEN, 20.
1864.

CASTEL OFF LOUE.

Her bygiɳet a tretys
Þat is yclept Castel off loue,
Þat bisschop Grosteyʒt made ywis
For lewede mennes by-houe.

Þat good þenkeþ¹ good may do,
And God wol helpe him þerto;
For nas neuere good werk wrouʒt²
W¹-oute biginninge³ of good pouʒt;
5 Ne⁴ neuer was wrouʒt⁵ non vuel⁶ þing
Þat vuel⁶ pouʒt⁷ nas þe biginnyng.
God, Fader and Sone and Holigost,
Þat alle þig on eorþe sixt and wost,
Þat o God art and þrilli-hod⁸,
10 And þreo persones In on-hod⁹,
Wiþ-outen ende and biginninge¹⁰,
To whom we ouʒten oner alle þinge;
Worschupe¹¹ him wiþ trewe loue,
Þat kineworþe¹² kyng [is]¹³ vs aboue;
15 In whom, of whom, þorw whom beoþ
Alle¹⁴ þe goodschipes¹⁵ þ¹ we here i-seoþ.

¹ A. þencheþ. ² A. wrouht. ³ A. beginynge. ⁴ A. noi see Gloss.
⁵ A. wrouht. ⁶ Vuel—In which doubtless the v is the vowel and u the
consonant—is the common form in V., as Mr. Wright prints uvel in his
edition of the Owl and Nightingale; except where he gives vrk = vvle
= uvle. A. begins the word always with e, euel. ⁷ A. þouht. ⁸ II.
triulté. ⁹ II. unité. ¹⁰ A. biginynge. ¹¹ A. worschipe. ¹² II.
crowynd. ¹³ II. ys, A. and V. art. ¹⁴ V. al. ¹⁵ II. goodnesses.

CASTEL OFF LOUE.

He leue vs þencho¹ and worchen so,
þat he vs schylde² from vre fo.

 Alle we habbeþ to help neode,
20 þat³ we ne beþ⁴ alle of one þeode,
Ne i-boren in one londe,
Ne one speche vnderstonde⁵;
Ne mowe we alle Latin wite,
No Ebreu⁶ ne Gru þat beþ i-write,
25 Ne French⁷, ne pis oþer⁸ spechen
þat me mihte in world sechen.
To herie God, vre derworþe drihte,
As⁹ vche mon ou3te¹⁰ w⁴ al his mihte,
Lof-song¹¹ syngen to God jerne
30 Wiþ such speche as he con lerne,
No monnes moaþ ne be¹² i-dut,
Ne his ledene¹³ i-hud¹⁴,
To sernen his God þ⁴ hi wrou3te¹⁵,
And maade¹⁶ al þe world of nou3te¹⁷.

¹ A. þenchen.   ² A. schilde.   ³ H. reads thauegh, to which þat is here equivalent: see Gloss.   ⁴ A. beoþ.   ⁵ A. vndurstonde.   ⁶ A. Ebreuh.   ⁷ A. Frensch.   ⁸ A. oþur. The n of spechen and sechen is half erased in A.   ⁹ H. omits as.   ¹⁰ A. ouhte.   ¹¹ V. loft song: H. looving to synge.   ¹² A. beo.   ¹³ A. leodene. As the A.S. hyden was undeclined, and no form exists in which it assumed an additional syllable, there is apparently no authority for sounding the final e of ledene, especially as a vowel follows. The reading in H. suggests a suspicion that the line should run—
    Ne his leden be i-hud;
but taking it as it stands we may scan thus:—
    Né | his lé | dén | i-húd:
compare 497 and 513, and Reineke de Fos (18 Kap.)—
    So | hyrfor | is | gesagd.
Or, still with fourfold ictus, (see Pr., pp. 59, 60)—
    Né his léden I-húd,
like l. 755, and nearly like Coleridge's Christabel, l. 5—
    How drowsily it crew.
¹⁴ H. gives this couplet thus:—
    No mones ay ne be adrede,
    Ne his ledene shall not be hed.
On this whole passage see Pr., p. 62.
¹⁵ A. wrouhte.   ¹⁶ A. made.   ¹⁷ S. nouhte.

85 On¹ Englisch² I chul mi³ resun⁴ schoweu
For hī þat con not I-knowen
Nouþer⁵ French ne Latyn:
On Englisch I challe tellen him
Wherfore þe world was i-wrouht,
40 And aftur⁶ how⁷ he was bi-tauht
Adam vre fader to ben his,
Wiþ al þe merþe⁸ of paradys⁹,
To wonen and welden to such ende,
Til þat he scholde to heuene wende;
45 And hou¹⁰ sone he hit for-les,
And seþþen¹¹ hou hit for-bouht¹² wes
þorw þe heiȝe¹³ kynges sone,
þat here on eorþe wolde come
For his sustren þ¹ were¹⁴ to-boren¹⁵,
50 And for a prison þ¹ was forloren;
And hou¹⁶ he made, as ȝe schul heeren,
þat heo I-custe and sauht¹⁷ weren;
And to wȝuche¹⁸ a Castel he alihte,
Þo he wolde here for vs ûhte:
55 Þat þe Marie bodi wes,
Þat¹⁹ he alihte and his in ches.

And tellen we schulen of Ysay²⁰,
Þat vs tolde trewely,
A child þer is i-boren to vs,
60 And a sone i-ȝiuen vs,

¹ A. in. ² The French is:—
En romanz comenz ma reison,
Por cans ki ne sonent mie
Ne lettrure ne clergie.
³ A. my. ⁴ A. reson. ⁵ A. noupur. ⁶ A. and aftor; V. þer-aftor;
H. and therafter. ⁷ A. hon. ⁸ A. murþe. ⁹ A. paradis. ¹⁰ A. how.
¹¹ After sethen H. inserts shall here—a verb without any nominative.
¹² A. forbouȝt. ¹³ A. hiȝe. ¹⁴ A. waere. ¹⁵ H. reads thus:—
But ther werene fowre systren i-boren
For a prisoner &c.
¹⁶ A. how. ¹⁷ A. sauȝt. ¹⁸ A. whnch. ¹⁹ H. therin: the true reading is perhaps þer, but see Gloss. s. v. þat. ²⁰ A. Ysaye.

CASTEL OFF LOUE.

Whos¹ nome schal i-nempned beon²
Wonderful, as me may i-seon³,
And God milbful and rihtwys;
Of þe world þat comen is
65 Lord þe Fader,⁴ and Prince of Pes⁵.
Alle þeos⁶ nomen hou he wes,
Je schulen⁷ I-heren and i-witen.
And of domes-dai hou hit is i-writen,
And of heuene we schulen telle,
70 And sūdel of þe pynen⁸ of helle.

Þauh⁹ hit on Englisch be dim¹⁰ and derk,
Ne nabbe no sauer¹¹ bi-fore a¹² clerk,
For lewed men þat luitel connen¹³,
On Englisch hit is þus bi-gonnen¹⁴.
75 Ac whose is witer¹⁵ and wys of wit,
And jerne¹⁶ bi-holdeþ þis ilke writ,
And con þat muchel of lintel¹⁷ vn-louken,
And hony of þe harde ston souken,
Alle poyntes he fynde may
80 Of vre be-leeue and Godes lay¹⁸;
Þat bi-falleþ to Godes godhede
As wel as to his monhede.
Ofte je habbeþ i-herd ar þis
Hou¹⁹ þe world I-maked is;

---

¹ A. hos. ² A. ben. ³ A. I-sen. ⁴ This punctuation seems to be justified, and indeed necessitated, by comparison with ll. 612, 613, and 1375, and with the French of that passage—

E deu, e fort, e ll pere
Du siecle ke uient apres.

The rendering of Is. 9. 6 in the Vulgate is as follows:—"Parvulus enim natus est nobis, et filius datus est nobis, et factus est principatus super humerum ejus; et vocabitur nomen ejus Admirabilis, consiliarius, Deus, fortis, pater futuri seculi, princeps pacis."
⁵ V. writes this as two lines, thus:—

Lord þe Fader
And Prince of Pes.

⁶ A. þeose. ⁷ A. schul. ⁸ ll. pyne. ⁹ A. þauȝ. ¹⁰ A. dym. ¹¹ A. saunr. ¹² A. omits a. ¹³ A. cunnen. ¹⁴ A. bignnnen. ¹⁵ A. ak hose is wyter. ¹⁶ A. jeorne. ¹⁷ V. luitel; A. and H. lintel. ¹⁸ H. lay. ¹⁹ A. how.

85 Forþi ne kep¹ I nouȝt to telle,
Bote þat² falleþ to my spelle.
In sixe dayes and sene niht
God hedde al þe world i-diht;
And þo al was derworþliche i-do
90 Þe seueþe day he tok reste and ro.

Lusteneþ to me, lordynges:
Þo God atte begynnynges³
Hedde i-maad⁴ heuene wiþ ginne,
And þe angeles so briht wiþ-inne,
95 And þe eorþe þer-after þer-wiþ,
And al þat euere in hiro bi-lyp⁵;
Lucifer in heuene wos so proud,
[þat]⁶ he was a-non i-cast out,
And mo angeles þe eni⁷ tonge mai telle
100 Fallen a-doun wiþ him to helle.
And ȝit was þe sonu þo seueþype⁸ I-wis
Brihtore forsoþe þen heo now is;
Also schon þe mone a-niht
So dop þe sone on day-liht.
105 Ne holde ȝe hit not⁹ for folye,
For so seiþ þe propheto Ysaye:
Alle þe schaftes þat þo weren¹⁰
More miȝt¹¹ and strengþe beren¹²
Bi-fore þat Adam þe world for-les.
110 Allas wjuch¹³ serwe and deol¹⁴ þer wes!

¹ A. keep.   ² bote þat = except what; as in the French, l. 40, (I quote from the MS.),

Asses souent oi aues
Comët le mund fa cries,
Por co ne vail Jo mie escrire
For co hapent a ma matire,
Ken als lors deu tut cria
Al setime se reposa.

³ A. at þe biginnynges.   ⁴ A. I-mad.   ⁵ A. hi-libþ.   ⁶ H. that,
V. and A. and: these four lines, "Lucifer .... to helle", are not in the French.   ⁷ A. angls þen eny.   ⁸ A. seuh siþe.   ⁹ A. omits not.
¹⁰ A. weoren.   ¹¹ A. miht.   ¹² A. beeren.   ¹³ A. whuch.   ¹⁴ A. del.

Alle heo beoþ i-brouht¹ to grounde
þat of his ofspringe² beoþ i-founde:
Of heuene-blisse heo beoþ i-flemed,
And to deolful deþ i-demed³.
115 þe reson is good and feir for-whi,
As I chulle ow telle for-þi,
þat ȝe schule loue God þe more⁴
And him seruen and clepe to his ore.

þo God hedde al þe world i-wrouȝt⁵
120 þat þer ne faykede riȝt⁶ nouȝt⁷,
Beest ne fisch ne foul to fleon
And vche þing as hit ouȝte to beon,
Bloame on bouȝ⁸ and breer⁹ on rys,
And alle þing betere¹⁰ þen hit nou is;
125 And þo he hedde al wel i-don¹¹,
He com to þe valeye of Ebron.
þer¹² he made Adam [and-last]¹³ so riche
Of corþe, after hym self i-liche;

¹ V. i-broub.   ² A. ofspring.   ³ A. i-deemed.   ⁴ Fr. has—
  E co par bone reison
  Apres nos dirai la cheison.
  Kar bon est le remēbrer
  Par deu plus chierement amer.
⁵ A. l-wrouht.   ⁶ A. riht.   ⁷ A. nouht.   ⁸ A. bouh.   ⁹ A. brer.
¹⁰ A. betire.   ¹¹ H. and though hede alle welle done.   ¹² Sir John
Maundevile in speaking of Hebron says: 'And righte faste by that Place
is a Cave in the Roche, where Adam and Eve dwelleden, whan thei weren
putt out of Paradyse; and there goten thei here Children. And in that
same Place was Adam formed and made; aftre that som men seyn. . . .
And fro thens was he translated in to the Paradys of Delytes, as thei
seyn, &c.' Compare the lamentation of Roberte the Deuyll:
     'Synce Adam was made in Canaan of claye
     I am the greatest synner that lyued on grounde.'
And,   'In þe vale of eboir &c.', Early English Poems, III, 37.   But
Chaucer (Monkes Tale) follows Lydgate and Boccaccio in placing the
creation of Adam 'In the feld of Damassene'.   ¹³ A. and V. and lafl,
H. at the last, and so Fr. has—
          Kant leo tresint fet a
          Tut auderaie adam cria.
See Cotgrave, s. v. derrain, and Gloss., s. v. and-last.

CASTEL OFF LOUE.   7

And aftur his holy prilli-hod
130 He schop his soule feir and good.
How' mi)te² be him more loue schowen
þen his oune liknesse habbē and owen?

To paradys' he ladde him þo,
And caste sleep on him also
135 þat of his syde a rib he nom,
And þer-of Eue his feere com.
He ȝaf Adam Eoe to wyue
To helpen;⁴ he ȝaf him wittes fyue⁵
To delen þat vnel⁶ from þe good⁷.
140 ȝif he wel him⁸ vnderstood⁹,

He ȝaf him ȝit more worschipe;
Of al þe world þe lordschipe,
And alle þe schaftes of water and lond
Scholden ben vnder¹⁰ his hond;
145 Feirlek, and freodam¹¹, and muche miht,
And þe world to delen and diht,
And paradys to wonen in
Wiþ-outen wo and serwe and pyn,
Wiþ-onten deþ in goode¹² lyue
150 þer Joye and blisse is so ryue;
And euere to libben i-liche ȝong,
O¹³ þat of hem to weren at-sprong¹⁴

---

¹ A. hou. ² A. mihte. ³ A. pardys. ⁴ A stop at *helpen* is necessary, though it gives a cæsura not common in this poem: the French is,
E puis deuant li lamena
E en aie lui dona.
⁵ A Tract attributed to Wicliffe begins thus: "Clerkys knowen that a man hath fiue wittes outward, and other fiue wittes inward." See Apol. for Loll. (Camd. Society), Intr. p. xv. With the present passage compare ll. 1173-1177. ⁶ A. euel. ⁷ A. gode. ⁸ A. him wol. ⁹ A. vndurstoode. ¹⁰ A. vndur. ¹¹ A. fredam. ¹² A. gode. ¹³ See Gloss. s. v. O; II. has 'and all tho that of hem two spronge', the writer evidently not knowing o in this sense. ¹⁴ V. and sprong.

þe noombre of þe soule þ' frõ heuene felle
þorw Lucifer a-donn to helle¹.
165 And whan hit forþ com at þe stren²,
So briȝt³ heo scholden i-blessed ben
So was þe sonne, as I er tolde,
Brihtore þen heo now⁴ is seuen folde⁵;
And so heo scholden to heuene wende,
160 To þe blisse wiþ-outen ende,
Wiþ-outen drede of depes dome.
And al þe of-spring⁶ þat of hem come,
From þat ilke day to þis,
Scholde so steyȝen to heuene-blis,
165 To þe heritage of wynne⁷ and wele⁸
Among þe murþe of aungeles⁹ fele¹⁰.

Two lawen Adam scholde i-wis
Witen and holden in paradis.
Þ' on him was þorw kynde¹¹ i-let:
170 Þat oþer¹² was clept lawe i-set.
Þat on him tauȝte¹³ atte leste
Þorw kynde¹¹ to holden Godes heste.
Þat oþer lawe [was]¹⁴ þat him was set:
"Of þe appel þow neuer ne et,

¹ Compare—
  har etides for to ful fille. þat wer i-falle for prude an hore:
  god makid adam to is wille. &c.   Early Engl. Poems, III, 17.
² A. streon.   ³ A. briht.   ⁴ A. nou.   ⁵ These three lines seem to mean: 'They should be glorified so bright as the sun was (then), as I before said, (that is to say) seven times brighter than she is now.' The French of the whole passage is as follows:—
    Pus feussent glorifies
    Tut sans murir (nel dotes)
    Si beaus, si clers, san tormaus,
    Come-fu lores li solaus,
    Si com auant vus ai contés;
    E pus el ciel fensssent mûte.
⁶ A. ospring.   ⁷ A. winne.   ⁸ A. weole.   ⁹ A. angeles.   ¹⁰ A. feole.
¹¹ A. kayude bis.   ¹² A. oþnr.   ¹³ A. tauhte.   ¹⁴ V. and A. omit was, which U. has and the sense demands.

175 Of þe tre¹ þat is for-bode."
So [him]² seide [and]³ hiȝte Gode,
Þat whon he of þe appel ete,
Þorw dep he scholde þe lyf for-lete;
And al þe kynde⁴ þat of him com⁵
180 Scholde þole þulke dom⁶;
And ȝif he heolde his beste riht,
God ȝaf him so muche miht
To welden al þis worldes winne
Wiþ-outen wo and serwe and sinne.

185 Þo seisyn⁷ hedde Adam þo
To wonen in blisse euere and o.
In muche murþe and joye he wes:
A-wei to sone he hit for-les,
His worschipe and his wel-fare,
190 [And]⁸ brouȝto⁹ vs alle in muche care.
Þo he of þe appel eet,
Godes heste he to-brek¹⁰,
Þe kuyndeliche and þe set ek¹¹.
Boþe his lawen¹² he to-breek,
195 And raþere he dude his wyues bode,
Þen he heold þe heste of Gode.

Þus Adam þorw reuþful rage
Was cast out of his heritage,
And out of paradys i-driue¹³,
200 In swynk and swot I world to liue.
Þe blisse of lyf he haþ forsaken,
And to deolful deþ him¹⁴ taken¹⁵.

¹ A. treo. ² H. hym, A. and V. he. ³ H. and, A. and V. þat.
The copyist of these MSS. has written as another man's words what it
is inconceivable that the translator should have written as his own; 'So
he who was called God said'. So I follow H. See Pr., pp. 62-64.
⁴ A. kuynde. ⁵ A. coom. ⁶ A. doom. ⁷ A. seysin. ⁸ H. and,
which V. and A. omit. ⁹ A. brouhte. ¹⁰ A. to-breek. ¹¹ A. eek.
¹² A. lawes. ¹³ A. i-dryne. ¹⁴ V. omits him. ¹⁵ V. i-taken.

Carfuliche¹ he haþ i-coren:
Now² he þorw rijt³ haþ i-loren
205 þe murþe þat he mijte⁴ hauen.
Whom mai⁵ he to helpe crauen?
Out of his heritage he is pult
For synne and for his owne⁶ gult.

Lucifer gon wel lyke þo,
210 þo Adam was bi-swiken so⁷;
For alle þe fendes hedden onde
þat he scholde come to þ¹ blisful londe
þat he hedde þorw pruide for-lore:
Wel hit likede⁸ hem þer-fore.
215 So muche wox beore miht þo,
þat al þe world moste after hem go;
And whon mon hedde i-lined⁹ in care,
Atte laste he moste dyen and forþ-faro¹⁰,
Ne mijte¹¹ him helpe no good dede
220 þat his soule moste to helle needo;
For so hit was þo¹² Adam bi-speke,
And God nolde no forward breke.

For eyle and hard and muche hit wes
þe synne þ¹ pus þe world for-les,
225 þat vche þing vnder heuene-driht
So muche les of strengþe and miht.
God ne wrouhte¹³ neuer þat þing
þat out-les þorw His wonyng;
For nis no wone on him i-long,
230 3if synne nere¹⁴ so hard and strong¹⁵.
For God jaf vche þing al his riht,
Ac¹⁶ sune¹⁷ wonede beore alre miht;
For suno¹⁷ and wone al is on.
And wone dude Adam þo anon,

¹ A. carefuliche. ² A. non. ³ A. riht. ⁴ A. mihte. ⁵ A. may.
⁶ A. onne. ⁷ II. has, That Adam had trespast so. ⁸ A. lyked. ⁹ A.
i-lyued. ¹⁰ A. forfare. ¹¹ A. mihte. ¹² II. to. ¹³ A. wroujte. ¹⁴ A.
neore. ¹⁵ A. stronge. ¹⁶ A. ah. ¹⁷ A. synne bis.

235 þo he Godes heste at-seet,
And eke þo he þe appel eet.
þorw wone he lees¹ his seysyne:
þorw wone he brouhte² hī-self in pyne.
In þe kynges court jit vche day
240 Me veeþ pulke selue lay³.

¹ A. les.   ² A. brouȝte.   ³ The sense of this difficult passage, from l. 227, appears to be as follows: 'God never created any thing which incurred forfeit through his fault (i. e., through God's fault, compare l. 653); for there is no fault attributable to Him—only sin is so hard and strong! For God gave to every thing all its powers; but sin made faulty (or, impaired) the qualities of them all (i. e. of all created things), for sin and fault are all one. And Adam committed a fault then in the very fact (see Gloss., s. v. Anon) that he set aside God's commandment (compare the Psalmist's words, The thought of foolishness is sin), and also when he ate the apple. Through his fault he lost his possession; through his fault he brought himself into suffering. In the King's court they still use this same law every day.' The French, of which our translator has given a loose and inaccurate rendering, runs thus:—

Trop fu grief iceu pechie
Kant trestut fent entuschie,
Kanque de sus le ciel fu
En perdi part de sa uertu,
155 Den ue fist chose si haute
Nahessast pa sa defaute,
Ke terriene chose feust
Chescune chose son dreit eust,
Ne feust pechie que tant grieue
160 Pechie a parole hriene,
Cest defaute apertement
Defaute e peche en vu sextent, &c.

Lines 155, 156 in the other French text stand thus:

Den ue fist chose si haute
Que ue hessast per defaute;

and the meaning, which the translator has quite mistaken, is clearly—'God made nothing so high that it was not brought down by his (i. e. Adam's) transgression.' ll. gives,

God whrowght never that thyng
But hit peyred thowrgh his wonning;
But for the wonning of him hit was not long;
Nere that synne was so hard and strong.

The first two of these lines follow the French: the meaning of the other two and those which follow it is very hard to conjecture.

Now is Adam wiþ wo i-nome:
Sūnes¹ þral he is bi-come,
Þat freore² was or þan eny þing
Þat liuede vnder heuene-kyng.
245 He is þorw riht þeowe and þral,
To whos seruise³ he vnderstod w'-al,
Whon he him serwede in [þewdome]⁴,
And [dede]⁵ wiþ-oute fredome.
And þeowe and þral may⁶ not craue
250 Þorw riht non heritage to haue:
As sone as he is þral bi-come,
His heritage is him bi-nome.
In court ne in none londe
Me ne ouȝte onswere hī ne vnderstonde⁷.

255 Þēne he mot a-noþer seche,
For to⁸ schewe⁹ for him his speche,
Þat mowe his heritage craue,
And þat he þe kynde haue;
Þat he beo i-boren fre,
260 And þat he ne eete¹⁰ of þe tre;
Þat he habbe i-wust wiþ-inne¹¹
Þe preo lawen wiþ-outē synne,
Þulke two of Paradys,
And þulke of þe Monnt Synays,
265 Þat to Moyses i-ȝiuen was,
Þat neuer ȝute i-holde nas
Of non þat euer dude sūne¹².
Who mihte þenne such mon mūne¹³
Oþer¹⁴ þenchen or i-knowe,
270 Þat such wonder mihte¹⁵ schowe?

¹ A. synnes. ² A. freor. ³ A. seruyse. ⁴ H. has thewdome, A.
and V. þe dome; the French is—
    Pus kil se selt en seruage
(sic MS.), which seems to mean, 'Since he placed himself in servitude'.
⁵ So H., V. diȝede, A. dyede. Fr. gives no help. ⁶ A. mai. ⁷ A.
vndnrstode. ⁸ A. forte. ⁹ H., That myȝht awowe. ¹⁰ A. ete. ¹¹ H.
with wynne. ¹² A. synne. ¹³ A. myne. ¹⁴ A. oþur. ¹⁵ A. myhte.

CASTEL OFF LOUE.

Siggen I may in þis stude
þerof þat ich er dude,
For nou Ichul tellen of þe stryf¹
þat a-mong þe foure sustren liþ².

275 Hit was a kyng of muche miht,
Of good wille and gret in-siht;
And þis kyng hedde a sone
Of such wit and of such wone,
Of such strengþe and of such chore,
280 As was his fader in his manere³.
Of on wille heo weoren bo,
And of on studefastschipe also;
Of on fulnesse heo weoren out-riht,
And boþe heo weoren of on miht.
285 Þorw þe sone þe fader al be-gon⁴
þat bi-lay to his kynedom⁵.
[What þat was of]⁶ his begynnynge⁷,
Þe fader wolde to ende bringe.

Foure douhtren⁸ hedde þe kyng,
290 And to vchone sunderlyng
He jaf a dole of his fulnesse,
Of his miht and of his wysnesse,
As wolde bi-fallen to vch-on;
And jit was al þe folnesse on
295 þat to him-self bi-lay,
Wiþ-oute whom he ne mai⁹

¹ A. strif.   ² A. lyþ.   ³ A. maneere.   ⁴ A. bi-gon.   ⁵ A. kyngdom.
⁶ V. and A. have, 'wiþ wit was &c.', leaving the verb 'bring' without
an object; II., 'alle that was of &c.' Hence it is not difficult to conjecture
the true reading, which the writer of II. changed from ignorance of the
common use in early English of þat after another relative pronoun. See
Gloss., s. v. þat. The French is,
    Quankil uoleit comencelr
    Par son fiz le uout cheuelr.
(Uout = voulut: Mr. Cooke prints vout, wrongly.) For the change of
þat into wit see note on l. 1401.   ⁷ A. biginnynge.   ⁸ A. doujtren.
⁹ A. may.

His kindom wiþ poes¹ wysen,
Ne wiþ rihte hit justisen.

 Good is to nempnen hem for-þi:
300 Þe furste douȝter hette Merci,
Þe kynges eldeste² douȝter heo is;
Þ' oþer³ hette Soþ i-wis;
Þe pridde soster⁴ is cleped Riȝt⁵;
Pees⁶ hette þe feorþe a-pliȝt⁷.
305 Wiþ-outen þeos foure wiþ worschipe
Mai⁸ no kyng lede gret lordschipe.

Þis kyng, as þou herdest ar þis,
Hedde a pral þat dude amis,
Þat for his gult strong and gret
310 Wiþ his lord was so i-vet,
Þat þorw be-siht of riht dom⁹
To strong prison was i-don,
And bi-taken to alle his fon
Þat sore him pyneden euerichon,
315 Þat of no þing heo nedden onde¹⁰
Bote¹¹ hi to habben vnder¹² honde.
Heo him duden in prisun¹³ of deþ,
And pynedē hī sore wiþ-outen meþ.

  ¹ A. pas. ² A. eldest. ³ A. oþer. ⁴ A. suster. ⁵ A. riht. ⁶ (The French in the Caxton Society's edition is,
    La quarte soer ad avon pes,
where for *avun* read *axun*: 'the fourth sister has Peace *for her name*'.)
⁷ A. apliht. ⁸ A. may. ⁹ A. doom. ¹⁰ H. corrupts these two lines thus:
    And of noothing that hadyn *dowte*,
    But hadde him in here rowte.
The French is,
    Kar dautre rien nourët *envie*
    Fors kanoir ll en lur baillie;
where *avoir envie* is clearly used as in modern French, and as in Palsgrave's time it meant 'to have a luste to a thyng'. But as it is very doubtful whether *onde* can signify simple desire, it seems to be a necessary conclusion that the translator has here misunderstood the original.
¹¹ A. but. ¹² A. vndur. ¹³ A. prison.

DE MISERICORDIA.

Merci þat a-non i-seiþ:
320 Hit eode¹ hire herte swipe neih²,
Ne mai³ hire no pig lengore holde.
Bi-foren þe kyng comen heo wolde
To schewen forþ hire resoun,
And to dilyuere⁴ þe prisoun.
325 "Vnderstond,"⁵ quaþ heo, "Fader myu,
Þou wost þat I am douþer þyn,
And am ful of boxumnes⁶
Of milce and of swetnes,
And al Ich habbe, Fader, of þe.
330 I be-seche⁷ þat þou⁸ here me,
Þat þe wrecche prisoun⁹
Mote come to sum rausum¹⁰,
Þat a-midden alle¹¹ his fon
In strong prison [þou]¹² hast i-don.

335 Heo hī made a-gulte pulke vn-wreste,
And bi-swikede hī þorw heor feir be-heste¹³,
And seiden him ȝif he wolde þe appel ete,
Þat whon he hedde al i-ete,

---

¹ Compare the expression in Reineke de Fos, p. 3,
    Men dat shândond mines wives—dat *gait* mi na—
    Blivt nigt ungewroken—wo it ok ga!
i. e., 'But the dishonouring of my wife—that touches me closely—shall
not remain unavenged, whatever happens.' And on p. 14,
    Ji sén it, wat he er hârt gedân:
    Dat latet ju dog *to hârte gân!*
² A. neiþ.   ³ A. may.   ⁴ A. diluere.   ⁵ A. vndurstond.   ⁶ A. buxomnes.   ⁷ V. beo seche.   ⁸ A. þow.   ⁹ We should have here a line of only five syllables, were we not warranted by the A. S. *wræcca* to sound the final syllable of *wrecché*.   ¹⁰ A. rausoun.   ¹¹ A. al.
¹² A. and V. omit þow; H. has 'In strong pyne *tho* hast him doon'; and Fr. gives—
    Ki onmi ses enemis
    Aues en grieno prison mis.
¹³ A. bi-beste.

16   CASTEL OFF LOUE.

           He scholde habbe al þe miht of Gode
       340 Of þe treo¹ þat him was for-bode;
           And be-gilede² hī þer-of, and heo luytel³
                                              rouȝte.
           For falshede euer-ȝite beo souhten⁴,
           And falshede⁵ hem i-ȝolde be,
           And þe wrecche prisun i-sold⁶ to me.
       345 For þow⁷ art kyng of boxumnes⁸
           Of milce and of swetnes⁹,
           And I þi douhter alre eldest¹⁰,
           Ouer alle þe opere¹¹ beldest.
           Neuer I þi douhter neore¹²,
       350 Dote¹³ milce toward him were.
           Milce and merci he schal haue:
           þorw milce I chulle þe prisun¹⁴ craue
           For þin owne¹⁵ swete pite:
           I schal him bringe to sauete.
       355 Þi milce for him I crie euer-more,
           And haue of him milce and ore.¹⁶

                       DE VERITATE.

           A-non whon Soþ þis i-seiȝ¹⁶,
           Hou Merci hire soster¹⁷ hir harte beiȝ¹⁸,
           And wolde þis pral of prisū¹⁹ bringe,
       360 Þat Riht bedde hī i-demd w³-outē ediȝe;

   ¹ A. tre.   ² V. be-gylen.   ³ A. luitel.   ⁴ A. souhton.   ⁵ A. falsede.
   ⁶ See Gloss., s. v. Sell.   ⁷ A. þou.   ⁸ A. boxumnesse.   ⁹ A. swetnesse.
   ¹⁰ Fr., as printed, l. 273, is—
                E jo la fille sui einsnee.
   It should be einsnee = aínée. The same expression occurs in l. 231 in
   the form eias nce.—In l. 276 (compare ll. 349, 350 of our text) there is
   a similar error:
                Ne dirrai ke la fille feusse
                Si de celui pitie neusse;
   where Mr. Cooke prints seusse. In the MS. the n and the u are frequently undistinguishable.   ¹¹ A. oþer.   ¹² A. nere.   ¹³ A. bul.
   ¹⁴ A. prison.   ¹⁵ A. oune.   ¹⁶ A. i-seih.   ¹⁷ A. suster.   ¹⁸ A. beih.
   ¹⁹ A. prison.

Al heo chaunged hire mood,
And bi-foren þe kyng heo stood.
"Fader, I þe biseche, herkne to me;
I ne may for-bere to telle hit þe
365 Hou hit me þinkeþ a wonder þing
Of¹ Merci my suster wilnyng,
Þat wolde w² hire milsful³ sarmon³
Diliuere⁴ þe þral out of prison⁵,
Þat swiþe⁶ a-gulte per Ich hit seih,
370 And tolde hit to Riht þ' stood⁷ me neih.

"Fader, Ich sigge þe for-þi,
Þou oubtest⁸ nouþt⁹ to heere¹⁰ Merci
Of no boone¹¹ þat heo bisecheþ þe,
Bote¹² Riht and Sooþ¹³ per-mide be.
375 And pow¹⁴ loucst Soþ and batest lees¹⁵,
For of þi fulnesse i-comen Ich wes.
And eke pow¹⁴ art kyng Riht-wys,
And Merci herte so reupful is
Þ' ȝif heo mai¹⁶ saue w² hire mylde speche
380 Al þat beo wole fore bi-seche,
Neuer schal be¹⁷ mis-dede a-bouht
And þ° kyng schall be¹⁷ douted riȝt¹⁸ nouht.

"Þou art also so trewe a kyng,
And stable of þouȝt in alle þyng¹⁹,

¹ See Gloss., and compare—
 Sire, a merveille thinke me
 Of Bowdewyns avouyng
 Ȝostyr euyn In the mnyng
 With-owtnn any lettyng
 Wele more thenns we thre.
   Avowynge of King Arther, 37. 5.
And Morte Arth. (Roxb. Cl.) p. 14,
 Wondir thoughti me nevir more
 Than me dyd of afolyd knight, &c.
² H. wylsfull. ³ A. sarmonn. ⁴ A. delynere. ⁵ A. prisonn.
⁶ H. suche; but compare l. 435. ⁷ A. stod. ⁸ V. onhtes. ⁹ A. not.
¹⁰ A. here. ¹¹ A. bone. ¹² A. but. ¹³ A. sop. ¹⁴ A. þᵃ bis.
¹⁵ A. les. ¹⁶ A. may. ¹⁷ A. beo bis. ¹⁸ A. riht. ¹⁹ A. þing.

18   CASTEL OFF LOUE.

385 For-þi me pinkeþ Merci wilneþ wonȝ¹
And spekeþ to-ȝeynes Riȝt² i-nouȝ³.
For Riht con hym⁴ in prisun þynde,
He ouȝte⁵ neuere⁶ milce to fynde;
Milce and merci he hap for-loren,
390 He⁷ was warned þer-of⁸ bi-foren.
Whi scholde me helpe pulke mon,
Þat nedde of hiself pite non?
His dom he mot habbe, as Soþ con sugge,
And al his mis-dede a-hugge."

DE JUSTICIA.

395 Riht i-herde þis talkyng:
Anon heo stod bi-foro þe kyng.
"Þi douȝter"⁹, heo seiþ, "I am, I wot bi þon,
For þou art kyng, riht domes-mon.
Þer beþ¹⁰ rihte domes mine,
400 Alle þine¹¹ werkes beþ ful of witte.
Þis þral of whö my sustren deeþ mene
Haþ [dom]¹² deserued¹³ as at ene¹⁴;
For ï tyme while þ' he freo wes,
He hedde w' him hoþe Merci and Pees¹⁵;
405 And Soþ and Riht he hedde ho,
And w' his wille he wente hem fro,
And tyed¹⁶ hym¹⁷ to wrappe and wouȝ¹⁸,
To wreccheddam¹⁹ and serwe i-nouȝ²⁰.

¹ A. wouh.   ² A. riht.   ³ A. i-nouh.   ⁴ A. him.   ⁵ A. oubte.
⁶ A. neuer. ⁷ A. and.   ⁸ A. her.   ⁹ A. douhter. ¹⁰ A. beoþ.
¹¹ A. þyne. ¹² So H.: Fr. is—
        Cit serfs dont parler ol
        Jugement ad deseral.
¹³ V. deseruet. ¹⁴ H. gives these two lines thus:
        This thralle of whom my sustren mevyn,
        Hath dome deserved, as þe jevȝn ·
(read ȝe-ȝevȝn rather, = Germ. gegeben, Tat. gigeban, &c.). For at ene
see Gloss. ¹⁵ A. pes. ¹⁶ A. tyþed. ¹⁷ A. him. ¹⁸ A. wouh. ¹⁹ A.
wrecchedam. ²⁰ A. i-nouh.

"So þat ȝif Riht geþ,
410 He schal euere þolyen¹ deþ;
For þo þow² him þe beste lijtest³,
þorw Soþ þᵃ [þen]⁴ þe deþ him diȝtest⁵,
And I my-self him ȝaf þe dom⁶
As sone as he hedde þe gult i-don;
415 For Soþ⁷ berþ witnesse þer-to,
And elles nedde I⁸ no dom i-do.
Ȝif he in court bi-foren vs were,
þo dom þⁿ scholdest⁹ sone i-here,
For Riht ne sparþ for to Jugge
420 What-so-euere Soþ wol sugge.
þorw wisdam heo demeþ alle
As wole to his¹⁰ gult bi-falle."

Soþ and Riht lo þus beo suggeþ,
And þis pral to deþe juggeþ.
425 Neuer nouþer ne spekeþ hī good,
Ne non [of hem]¹¹ merci vnderstood¹²,
Ac¹³ as a mon mis-i-rad
On vche half he is mis-bi-lad,
Ne helpeþ hī no þīg wher-so he wende¹⁴
430 þat his fo¹⁵ fetteþ¹⁶ hī in vche ende,

¹ A. þollen. ² A. þou. ³ A. hihtest. ⁴ V. and A. himᵢ II. reads,
Thorgh sothe then deth to him thou bettyst.
⁵ A. dihtest. ⁶ A. doom. ⁷ A. soop. ⁸ For nedds I II. reads
nedlyche. ⁹ A. schuldest. ¹⁰ A. and V. his—a manifest solecism after
the plural alle: II., mindful of syntax though not of prosody, gives the
line thus:
Aftur here gult, as his heore doth befalle.
Fr. has the singular construction in both lines:
A chescun done por saueir
Quonkil doit par droit aueir.
¹¹ So II.: A. and V. þat. ¹² A. vnderstod. ¹³ A. ah. ¹⁴ A. weende.
¹⁵ II. foon, but Fr. has the sing., like A. and V. both here and in L 434,
he dude. ¹⁶ II. fyhtyth, and this fetteþ, if it is the true reading,
must mean the same. Fr. has—
Ne se pent garir on kil ant
Kel enemi nel assant,
'he cannot help himself, wherever he goes, but that the enemy attacks
him'. See Gloss.

And [haþ]¹ i-strupt him al start naked²,
Of miȝt³ and strengþe al bare i-maked⁴.
Him and al⁵ þat of him sprong
He dude a þenwedam vyl and strong,
435 And made a-gult swiþe i-lome
And Riht com after⁶ wiþ hire dome.
Wiþ-outē Merci and Pees⁷ heo con jugge
Euer aftur þat Soþ wol sugge.
Ne Pees mot not mid hem be⁸,
440 Out of londe heo mot fle⁹,
For Pees bileueþ in no londe
Wher þat¹⁰ is werre, nuy, and onde.
Ne Merci mot not a-mong hem liue,
Ac¹¹ boþe heo beþ¹² of londe i-driue.

445 Nis þer nout in world bi-leued
Þat nis destrued¹³ and to-dreued,
And dreynt, for-loren, and for-demed,
But eiȝte¹⁴ soulen þ¹ weren¹⁵ i-ȝemed
In þe schup; and þat weoren heo,
450 Noe and his sones þreo
And heore wyues þ¹ heo hedden bi-fore:
Of al þe world nas be-leued¹⁶ more.
Careful herte him ouȝto¹⁷ come
Þat þencheþ vppon þe dredful dome;
455 And al hit is þorw Riht and Soþ,
Þat wiþ-outen Pees and Merci doþ.

DE PACE.

So þat Pees a-last vp-breek,
And þus to hire Fader speek:

¹ A. and V. omit the auxiliary, though necessary with the participle
i-strupt; II. reads,
          And Aʒn stripte him alle start naked.
² A. naket.   ³ A. miht.   ⁴ A. l-maket.   ⁵ A. and V. al; see Gloss.
⁶ A. aftur.   ⁷ A. pes.   ⁸ A. beo.   ⁹ A. fleo.   ¹⁰ A. þat, V. þer; but
the latter is probably an error of the scribe, as this use of þer (as in
there is = Fr. il y a) is rarely found in this text.   ¹¹ A. ak.   ¹² A.
beoþ.   ¹³ A. distruyied.   ¹⁴ A. eihte.   ¹⁵ A. weoren.   ¹⁶ A. bi-leued.
¹⁷ A. ouhte.

CASTEL OFF LOUE.   21

"I am þi douȝter sauȝt and some,
460 And of þi fulnesse am i-come.
To-fore þe my playnt I make:
Mi two sustren me habbeþ forsake;
Wiþ-outen me heo doþ heore dom¹,
Ne Merci among hem nouȝt ne com².
465 For no pig þat I miȝte do,
Ne moste Merci hem come to³;
Ne for none kunnes fey⁴
Ne moste ich hem come neyȝ⁵.
Ak⁶ þat dom is al heoro owen;
470 For-þi Ich am⁷ of londe i-flowen,
And wole wiþ þe lede my lyf
Euer on⁸ þat ilke stryf
Þat a-mong my sustren is a-wake,
Þorw sauhtnesse⁹ mowe eū ende take¹⁰.

475 "Ac what is hit euer þe bet.
Þat Riht and Sop ben i-set,
Bote heo witū wel þe pees¹¹?
Rihtes mester¹² hit is and wes
In vche dom Pees to maken:
480 Schal I penne beo¹³ forsaken,
Whon eueriche¹⁴ good fourme¹⁵ is wrouht,
And to habben me bi-þouht¹⁶?
Ak¹⁷ he ne louede [me]¹⁸ neuere¹⁹ to fere,
Þat Merci my suster nul not here.

¹ A. doom.   ² A. coom.   ³ A. come hem to.   ⁴ A. feiȝ.   ⁵ A. nelȝ.
⁶ A. ac.   ⁷ A. I am.   ⁸ on in both MSS.: see Gloss., s. v. on.   II.
reads tyll.   ⁹ A. sauȝtnesse.   ¹⁰ A. maket II. reads 'mowe so ende
take'.   ¹¹ V. pees without þe.   ¹² See Pr., p. 54, and Gloss. s. v.   ¹³ A.
be.   ¹⁴ A. eueri.   ¹⁵ fourme as one word in both MSS., of course = for
me: compare mitte = mid the = with thee, l. 399.   ¹⁶ A. bi-þouȝt.   ¹⁷ A.
ak, V. and, II. but. The French, of which we can scarcely call this
couplet a translation, is—
                Mes sauue ne su io mie
                Se misericorde nest oie.
¹⁸ II. gives the pronoun, omitted by A. and V., but sanctioned by the
French, and imperatively required by the sense: 'But he who will not
bear my sister Mercy, never loved me as his companion.'   ¹⁹ A. neuer.

485 "Of vs foure, Fader, I chul telle þe
Hou me þinkeþ hit ou͡te to be.
Whon þe foure beþ¹ to-gedere i-sent
To don an euene juggement,
And schal þorw skil alle and some
490 3iuon and demen² euene dome,
Þer ne ou͡te no dom forþ³ gon,
Er þen þe foure ben a-ton.
At-on heo moten at-stonden alle,
And loken seppen⁴ hou dom wol falle.

495 "Be⁵ vs foure þis I telle,
We beoþ not alle of on⁶ spelle:
Boþe⁷ Ich and Merci
We be-clepeþ þe dom for-þi;
Hit is al as Ri͡t⁸ and Soþ wol deme,
500 Merci⁹ ne me nis hit not qweme.
Wiþ-outen⁹ vs þer is bale to breme:
For-þi, Fader, þow nime¹⁰ ͡emc.
Of vche goodschipe¹¹ Pees¹² is ende,
Ne¹³ fayleþ no weole þer heo wol lende;
505 Ne wisdam¹⁴ nis not worþ an hawe,
Þer Pees fayleþ to felawe;
And hoso Pees loueþ wiþ-outen gabbe,
Pees wiþ-outen ende he schal habbe.
Mi word ou͡te ben of good reles,
510 For þou art Kyng and Prince of Pes.

¹ A. beoþ. ² A. deemen. ³ A. forth. ⁴ A. seppe. ⁵ A. beo. ⁶ A. one.
⁷ See Glms., s. v. Boþé. ⁸ A. riht. ⁹ These two lines are contained
in V. (Fr. and H.), but omitted in A. The French of this passage is,
Cest Ingement iert repeles
Ke sanz nus niert pas iuges,
Sanz uns est trop flaeles
Par co doit tronsir pities:
that is, 'This judgment shall be revoked, so that it shall not be decided
without us: without us he is too severely punished: for this cause he
ought to find pity.' (For flacles = scourged, compare Wright's L. P.,
p. 77, 'e desconrges flaslé'.) ¹⁰ A. nyme. ¹¹ A. goodschups. ¹² A.
pes. ¹³ A. þer. ¹⁴ A. wisdom. H. reads, Wyt ne wisdam is not &c.
This line is not in the French.

"For-þi þou ouȝtest¹ to here me,
And Merci my suster þ¹ clepeþ to þe,
Þat þe pral þe prisoun
Mote come to sum ransoun.
515 Vre wille, Fader, þou do sone²,
And³ here vre rihte bone;
For Merci enere clepeþ to þe,
Til þat þe prison dilynered⁴ be,
And⁵ I chul fleon⁶ and neuere come,
520 Bote⁷ my sustren ben sanȝt and some."

Þe kynges sone al þis con heren⁸,
Hou his sustren hem to-beeren;
And seiȝ pis strif so strong awaken,
And Pees and Merci al forsaken,
525 Þat w¹-onten help of his wisdome
Ne⁹ mihten heo neuere to-gedere come.
"Leoue Fader", qnaþ¹⁰ he, "Ich am þi sone,
Of þi wit and of þi wone,
And þi wisdam¹¹ [me]¹² clepeþ me.
530 And so muche þou louedest me
Þat al þe world for me þou wrouȝtest¹³,
And so þou me in werke [brouȝtest]¹⁴;
For we beoþ¹⁵ on in one fulnesse,
In miht, in strengþe, and in helpnesse¹⁶:
535 I chulle al don þat þi wille is,
For þou art kyng rihtwis¹⁷.

"So muche, Fader, ich nyme ȝeme
Of þis strif þat is so breme,
Þat for þe tale þat Merci tolde þe
540 Ful sore þe prisun¹⁸ reweþ me:

¹ A. ouhtest. ² A. soone. ³ A. and Fader bere. ⁴ A. delynered. ⁵ A. for,
Fr. e. ⁶ A. fleo. ⁷ A. but. ⁸ A. heeren. ⁹ A. heo mihte neuer &c.
¹⁰ A. qd. ¹¹ A. wisdom. ¹² A. and V. omit me; H., mrn; Fr., is
sapience sui clame. ¹³ A. wrouhtest. ¹⁴ A. bouhtest, V. bouȝtest, H.
browghtest, which the sense demands. ¹⁵ A. beþ. ¹⁶ A. helhnesse.
¹⁷ A. rihtwys. ¹⁸ A. prison.

For-þi he rewaþ me wel þe more,
For Merci euere clepeþ þin ore.
Þou art, Fader, so milsful¹ kyng,
Hire we schul heren of alle þing.
545 Al [hire wille I chulle]² done
And sauhten Soþ and hire ful sone.

"Nimen I chulle þe pralles weden⁸,
As Soþ and Riht hit wolden and beoden⁴.
And al-one I chul holde þe doom⁵,
550 As justise ouhte⁶ to don;
And maken I chulle⁷ Pees to londe come,
And Pees and Riht cussen and be sauȝt and
some,
And druynen⁸ out werre, nuy, and onde⁹,
And sauen al þe folk in londe."

555 Hose þis forbysene¹⁰ con,
He may openliche i-seo bi þon
Þat al þis ilke tokenynge
Is Godes in-sibt, Almihti Kynge¹¹.
Wiþ God þe Fader nis maked nouht¹²,
560 Þorw God þe Sone is al þing wrouht,
And alle þing is folfuld¹³ out-riht
Þorw God þe Holigostes miht¹⁴.

¹ A. mihtlful, II. makefulle.   ² A. and V. read, 'al þe schulen hire
wille done', which does not suit the context, and exhibits the false syntax
of 'al þe' for 'alle þe'. II. gives the converse of this grammatical error,
but has the right sense, 'alle here wyll I chull don', consistently with
Fr., 'trestut son noler fersi'.   ³ A. weeden.   ⁴ A. boden.   ⁵ A. dom.
⁶ A. oujte.   ⁷ V. chule.   ⁸ A. driuen.   ⁹ A. oonde.   ¹⁰ A. forbisene ɪ
II. has this line thus:
Who so this *afore bese* con.
¹¹ For the construction compare—'And in that Weye is the Tombe of
Rachelle that was Josephes Modrɪ the Patriarke'; Mandevile, p. 72. 'The
kyngys doghtur of Sodam'; Emp. Oct., l. 1097. 'This is launcelotts sheld
delake'; Mort Arth. (Roxb. Cl.), p. 21.   ¹² A. onjt, preceded by an
erasure.   ¹³ A. fulfild.   ¹⁴ In II. these four lines are thus strangely
metamorphosed:

And alle þreo beþ¹ on, þouh hit be so,
In one fulnesse and in no mo.
565 He ȝiueþ his blessynge w*t* mouþ and honde
To alle þat þis writ vnderstonde².

Ȝe habbeþ i-herd, as Ich ow³ tolde,
For-whi God þe world maken wolde,
And hou Adam for-les þorw synne
570 World and heuene, and al mon-kynne,
Þat for miȝt⁴ ne strengþe ne for no þing
No mon nedde of him-self a couryng;
Ne angel miȝte⁵ mon helpe on none wyse,
Ne mon miȝte⁶ hi-self fro deþe aryse.
575 Þene moste nede beo⁷ þorw vche doom⁸
Þat God of heuene mon bi-com;
Mon þe deþ þolen þorw serwen ryue,
And God vp-rysen from deþ to lyue:
Elles were⁹ alle for-lore to nouht
580 Þat God hedde in þe world i-brouht.

Herkeneþ⁹ [whuch]¹⁰ loue and bounnesse¹¹,
Whuch milce and eke swetnesse¹²,
Þat God from heuene [alihten]¹³ chees¹⁴
For o [sele shepe]¹⁵ þat he lees:
585 [Þe niti nine he leuede]¹⁶ and eode
To sechen on in vncouþ þeode.

Fadur withoute God is maked nowght,
Thorwgh God the Sone hath alle thing wrowght,
And alle thyng hath fulled atryȝht,
Thorgh Good the Holygostes myȝht.

¹ A. beoþ. ² A. vndurstonde. ³ A. ou. ⁴ A. miht. ⁵ A. mihte *his*.
⁶ A. be. ⁷ A. dom. ⁸ A. weore. ⁹ A. herkneþ. ¹⁰ A. and V. vchone;
II. wheche. ¹¹ A. boxunes. ¹² A. swenes. ¹³ A. and V. alihte and;
II., to alyȝht. ¹⁴ A. chees. ¹⁵ This is the reading of II.: A. and V.
have *mon*. ¹⁶ A. and V. þritti ȝeer he liuede; II. has this couplet thus—
His fadur blysse he leuede, and ther fro ȝeode
To seche theke shepe in uncouthe ȝode.
I have discussed this passage pretty fully in Pr., p. 63, but I may add,
by way of accounting for the apparently strange reading of A. and V.,

Þene nis þer such herde-mon non,
No non so miȝtful¹ lord as he is on.
Whose² wolde his herte on such lord holde,
590 Þat so muche loue hí knipe wolde,
Þat lyk him-self wolde him make,
Aud siþen deþ polyen for his sake;
Er him ouȝte þe herte to springe,
Þen he scholde hí wrappe for³ eny þinge⁴.

595 Herkeneþ now forþere atte frome
How⁵ vr Saueor⁶ wolde come.
To Abraham þe tiþinges comen,
Þe prophetes hit vnder-nomen⁷:
Þat is, Moyses and Jonas,
600 Abacuk and Helyas,
Daniel and Jeremye,
Dauid and Ysaye⁸,
And Eliseu⁹ and Samuel,
Siggeþ Godes comynge wel.
605 Wonder hit were hem alle to telle,
Ac¹⁰ herkeneþ hou Ysaye con spelle.

ᵃ quotation from the Harrowing of Hell, MS. Bodl. Digby 86, fo. 119.
Jesus is the speaker:

   Hard(e) gates hani gon
   Serewes soffred moni hon
   Þritti winter and half pritti ȝer
   Haui ben wend alende her.

(Alende = and lende = and dwelt.) I may also observe that in the second French text printed by the Caxton Society two lines of the six have dropped out, and the sense is marred accordingly: the other four, scarcely differing from those of Fr. 1, are—

   Ke deu du ciel descendi
   Por sowaylle kil perdi.
   Nonante et ir [read ix.] llessa
   Por one quere sen ala.

¹ A. mihtful. ² A. hose. ³ A. in. ⁴ H. reads these two lines thus:
   Sore he awght his handys to wrynge,
   That this Lord wold greve for enytbyng.
⁵ A. hon. ⁶ A. sauiour. ⁷ A. vndur-nomen. ⁸ A. Isaye. ⁹ V. Elisen. See Gloss. ¹⁰ A. ak.

CASTEL OFF LOUE. 27

PUER NAT' E' NOB' FILIU' DAT' EST NOBIS.

"A child per is i-boren to vs,
And a sone i-jeuen vs,
þat schal vp-holden his kynedome¹,
610 And al þus schal ben his nome,—
Wonderful² God, and of miht
And redeful³, and Fader ariht
Of al þe world þat her after schal ben⁴ ı
Prince of Pees me schal him sen⁵."
615 Þeos beþ⁶ þe nomen, as je mowe leeuen,
Þat þe prophetes him jeeuen⁷.

Ȝif je wolen⁸ heren⁹, tellen I chulle
How¹⁰ þat child is wonderfolle.
Such wonder nas neuer i-herd in¹¹ sawe,
620 Ne neuer schal bi none dawe
For no tyme þat euer schal come,
As God of heuene mon bi-come.
For hose now i-seje heere¹²
A child þat riht i-limed nere,
625 Þat preo feet and preo honde beere,
And a-noþer þat operweis weere¹³,
Þat hedde foot or hond for-lore,
And heo weore boþe so i-bore;

¹ A. kyngdome. ² A. wonderful. ³ II. rewfoll; but Fr. reads,
E son non nome serra.
Merueillus e cōseillere.
⁴ See note on l. 65. ⁵ A. seon. ⁶ A. beoþ. ⁷ A. jeuen. ⁸ A.
wole. ⁹ A. heeren. ¹⁰ A. hou. ¹¹ II. uy, i. e. 'such wonder was
never heard of nor seen', but saw = sees does not occur in this poem,
if it does anywhere else, not to say that we should much more naturally
say 'seen nor heard of' than 'heard of nor seen'. The phrase in our
text however is fully justified by the usage of early English writers.
Compare for instance Laȝ. Brut, vol. I, p. 284,
Wo lhorde euere segge:
a saȝe oþer spelle.
and again vol. III, p. 206,
Nes hit iseid numere:
as saȝe no on leoðe.
¹² A. here. ¹³ A. were.

28   CASTEL OFF LOUE.

　　　　Weoren¹ heo wonderfol², þeose two?
630　Nay forsoþe neoren heo no;
　　　　For þe on hedde kuynde oner mep,
　　　　And þat oþer to lnyte³, and so hit geþ.
　　　　Ac⁴ hit is as hit mot nedo ben,
　　　　Of vn-mete⁵ kuynde a forschipte streon⁶.

635　Ak þat mihte muche wonder ben,
　　　　Ȝif me miȝte⁷ eny i-seon
　　　　Þat monnes knynde bedde al aribt,
　　　　Þat hī neore to loite ne to muche wiht,
　　　　So þat he ware⁸ al sopfast mon,
640　Þat no forschippyng weore hī on,
　　　　And eke were⁹ good hors w¹ alle;
　　　　Such þing may neuer bi-falle.
　　　　For hose seȝe a such gederyng,
　　　　He mihte hit clepe a wonder þing.

645　And ȝit is more wonder a þousend folde
　　　　Of þe child þat Ysayȝe⁹ of tolde,
　　　　And clepede hī wonderful¹⁰ for þon,
　　　　Þat he is sop God and sop mon.
　　　　For of monhede ne wontep hī nonht,
650　And þorw him is al¹¹ þing i-wrouht;
　　　　And wiþ-outan [synne he is]¹² enere,
　　　　For wone [therof]¹³ dude he nanere;

¹ A. weore.　² A. wonderful.　³ A. luitel.　⁴ A. ah.　⁵ A. vn-meete.
⁶ Fr. puts this more briefly:
　　　　Meruellous ulerent la nomes
　　　　Mes mustres solent apeles.
When did *monster* in this sense first become an English word?
⁷ A. mihte.　⁸ A. weore bis.　⁹ A. Ysayo.　¹⁰ A. wondurfol.
¹¹ A. alle.　¹² So II.: A. and V. *him is synne*.　¹³ So II., and Fr. has the phrase 'en defaute', where I suspect the translator took *en* for the pronoun, and intended to convey the meaning that 'the defect or fault of it (i. e. of sin) be never committed'. But either I quite misunderstand the original, or he misunderstood it, as I think he did in the place to which lines 653, 654 allude, (see l. 228 of our text, and the note on l. 240). The French here runs thus:

CASTEL OFF LOUE.   29

No no schaft þorw him miȝte¹ lees,
As bi-foren i-rad wes.
655 Oþer God nis þen he þ' heuene dihte
Þat from henene dude alihte,
And vnder² vre wede vre kynde³ nom,
And al sop-fast mon bi-com.
And whon he wolde allen bi-come mon,
660 He moste be⁴ boren of a wommon,
Þulke schaft to vnderfonge⁵ wiþ-alle
Þat ouȝte to monnes kynde⁶ bi-falle.

       Plus merueille est uni itant
       La grant merueille del enfant.
       Ke ȝunie ad onncle
550   Kest nerrals hō e nerral de.
       Domanile ne li fant rien
       E kil est plein den co seū blé.
       Par lui tute riens est fet
       E sans li nnle rien nest.
555   Kar en defante nest pas fet
       Com auant nons al retret,
       Autre den nest nul for li
       Ki en terre descendi
       E de sus entre vesture
560   Pleinement prist la nature.
       De la nostre humanite
       E denint hōme en nerite.

The subject here treated of is the deity of Christ in conjunction with
his humanity. 'Of humanity he lacks nothing, and that he is very God,
that we see well. By him every thing is made, and without him nothing
is.' Then come two lines which our translator expands into four (651
to 654), and which he takes to refer to the sinlessness of Christ. The
couplet seems to me to be rather a parenthesis on the glory and com-
pleteness of the creation—'for it was not made defective (or, faulty) as
I have above reminded you'; (see ll. 101 to 109 of our text).—As to the
therof in this line, for the metre it seems almost indispensable. We may
possibly scan

              Fór | wòne | dúde | he nénere
which would be perhaps the worst line in the poem; but it is much
better thus :

              For wòne | theróf | dúde | be nénere.

¹ A. miȝhte.   ² A. vndur.   ³ A. kuynde bis.   ⁴ A. ben.   ⁵ A. vndurfonge.

God nolde alihte in none manere¹
But in feir stude and in² clere³;
665 In feir stude and clene siker hit wes,
Þor God almihti his in chees:
In a Castel wel comeliche,
Muche and feir and loneliche;
Þat is þo Castel of alle flonr,
670 Of solas and of socour.

In þe mere he stont bi-twene two,
Ne hap he ferlak for⁴ no so;
For þe tour is so wel wiþ-outen,
So depe⁵ i-diched al abouten,
675 Þat none konnes assaylyng
Ne may him dernen for no þing⁶.

He stont on heiȝ roche and sound,
And is i-planed i-to þe ground,
Þat þer ne mai⁷ wone non vuel⁸ þing,
680 Ne derne no gynnes⁹ castyng.
And þauȝ¹⁰ he be¹¹ so loneliche,
He is so dredful and hateliche
To alle þulke þat ben his fon,
Þat heo flen¹² hi cnerichon.
685 [Foure] smale toures [þer] beþ abouten¹³
To witen þe heiȝe tour wiþ-outen.

¹ A. maneere. ² A. omits *in*. ³ A. cleere. ⁴ A. of. ⁵ A. deope.
⁶ H. reads this couplet—
    That *no maner* assaylyng
    Ne may him *harme* for no thyng.
See note on L 855. ⁷ A. may. ⁸ A. euel. ⁹ A. ginnes. ¹⁰ A.
þauh. ¹¹ A. beo. ¹² A. fleon. This is one of the few passages in
which H. has preserved older forms than A. and V., having *fleth* for *flen*
in this line and *beth* for *ben* in the preceding. But the sense in H. is
sadly mangled, or rather utterly destroyed. The lines stand thus:
    And eke hit is so levelych,
    So dredfull and comlyche
    To alle tho that beth his foon,
    That thei fleth him everichon.
¹³ A. and V. read—
    For smale toures þat beþ (A. beoþ) abouten;

Seppe beoþ þre¹ Bayles wiþ-alle
So feir i-diht w¹ strong walle
As heo beoþ here-after i-write;
690 Ne may² no mon þe feirschipe i-wite,
Ne no tonge ne may hit telle,
Ne poujt³ þenche, ne moup spelle.

On trusti⁴ roche heo stondeþ faste,
And wiþ depe⁵ diches beþ⁶ bi-caste.
695 And þe camels so stondeþ vp-riht,
Wel i-planed and feir i-diht.
Seue berbicans per beoþ i-wrouht,
Wiþ gret ginne⁷ al bi-þouht,
And euerichon haþ jat and tour:
700 þer neuer ne faylep socour.

Neuer schal fo him stonde wiþ
þat þider wol flen⁸ to sechen grip.
þis Castel is siker and feir abonten,
And is al depeynted w¹-onten
705 Wiþ preo heowes þ¹ wel beþ⁹ sene;
So is þe foundement al grene,
þat to þe roche faste liþ⁹.
Wel is þat þer murþe i-sihþ;
For þe greneschipe lasteþ euere,
710 And his heuh¹⁰ ne leoseþ¹¹ neuere.
Seþþen abouten þat oþer¹² heu¹³
So¹⁴ is inde and eke bleu:

but fl. in reading *foure* and *ther* is confirmed by Fr.,
   Enuirun ad quatre toreles
   En tot le mod al a sibeles,
that is, 'Environ il a quatre tourrelles: dans tout le monde il n'y a pas de si belles.'

¹ A. þreo. ² A. mal. ³ A. þouht. ⁴ The Fr. has 'on the natural rock'—sur roche uaine. ⁵ A. deope. ⁶ A. beoþ *bis*. ⁷ A. gynne.
⁸ A. fleon. ⁹ A. lyþ. ¹⁰ A. heuj. ¹¹ ll. leseth: Fr., *pert*; see note 14.
¹² A. oþur. ¹³ A. henh. ¹⁴ To see the force of this so we must quote the French.

605 Li chasteaus est bel ebon
    De hors depeint enuiron.

Þat þe middel heuj¹ we clepeþ ariht,
And schyneþ so feire and so brijt².

715 Þe pridde heuj an³ onemast
Oner-wrijeþ al and so is i-cast
Þat wiþ-innen and wiþ-outen
Þe castel lihteþ al abouten,
And is raddore þē euere eny rose schal⁴,
720 Þat puncheþ as hit barnde al⁵.

        De .III. colors diuersement
        Si est uert le fundement.
        Ki a la roche se joint
   810 De grant decour ni faut point.
        Kar cele douce uerdour
        Ne pert iames sa colour.
        La color kest enmi lui
        Si reat e ynde. e blui.

That is to say, just as the green 'never loses its colour', so the colour that occupies the middle place '*in like manner remains*' an unfading blue, of which there are two shades, a darker and a lighter.

¹ A. heu.   ² A. briht.   ³ *An*, which is the reading of all the authorities, seems to be = *on*, which we have in l. 789. For *on* in this sense see l. 1488 and Coleridge's Glossarial Index. *Onemast* is evidently *overmost*, if we had such a word, so that the phrase clearly means '*on top*'. (We might, were it not for line 789, take this *onemast* as an adjective, as *onemast* is given in the Gloss. Ind. Then *on* will be = *and*, as often in Early English,—for example

        Even *on* morne both er thay wroght,

Towneley Mysteries, p. 2,—and as *an* for *unde* frequently in Old Saxon, —for example (Hein. de Foe, p. 1)

        — men de wolde *an* felde sag
        Grōne stān mid lōv *an* gras,
        Us männig fogel frolik was
        Mid sange in hagen *unde* up bomen.

But of *on* in this sense our poem has no second instance.)

⁴ Schal = shall be, see Glossary.   ⁵ The French of these six lines is—
        La tierce color par enson
        Les karneaus coure enuron.
        Plus est uermaille que nest rose
   620 E plert vne ardante chose.
        Tant reflambele enuiron
        Ke tot couers le dongon.

Wiþ-inne þe Castel is whit schinynge¹,
So² þe snow³ þat is sneuwynge⁴,
And casteþ þat liȝt⁵ so wyde
After-long⁶ þe tour and be-syde,
725 Þat neuer comeþ þer wo ne wouȝ⁷,
Ac swetnesse þer is euere i-nouȝ⁸.

Amidde þo heiȝe tour is sprigynge⁹
A wolle þat euere is eornynge
Wiþ foure stremes þat strikeþ wel,
730 And orneþ¹⁰ vppon þe grauel,
And fulleþ þe diches a-boute þo wal;
Muche blisse þer is ouer-al,
Ne dar he¹¹ seche non oper¹² leche,
Þat mai¹³ riht of his water¹⁴ cleche.

735 In þulke derworþe feire tour
Þer stont a trone wiþ muche honour,
Of whit iuori¹⁵, and feirore of liht
Þen þe someres day whon hee¹⁶ is briht¹⁷,
Wiþ compas i-þrowen and w' gin al i-do.
740 Seuene steppes þer¹⁸ beoþ þer-to,

The emeon here and in l. 691 is, I suppose, the Latin in summo, so that par-en-son is a phrase closely analogous to par-a-mount, par-a-vail, par-a-vans, par-de-hors, and other such.— Uermaille and tans — sic in MS.: Mr. Cooke prints merveille and tant.

¹ A. schininge.   ² A. as.   ³ A. snowb.   ⁴ A. sueuȝwynge.   ⁵ A. liht.   ⁶ A. afturlong.   ⁷ A. wouh.   ⁸ A. i-nouh.   ⁹ A. spriginge.
¹⁰ A. eorneþ.   ¹¹ V. dar he, A. þar him, the more usual expression. 11. paraphrases thus:
         That man nedeth non other leche.
¹² A. oþur.   ¹³ A. may.   ¹⁴ A. water.   ¹⁵ A. ynori.   ¹⁶ A. he.
¹⁷ In the French of this line, and of l. 629, for un read mi. Ken mi leste = qu'en mi(lieu de) l'été, cami being a word of similar formation to parmi, and found elsewhere though not given by Colgrave nor (as one word, which it really is) by Kelham. One other instance is in Wright's L. P. p. 65,
         Mon ostel est en mi la vile de Paris.
¹⁸ A. omits þer.

þat so feire w' ordre i-tiȝed¹ beoþ,
Feiror þing in world no mon seoþ;
For henene-honwe is abouten i-bent,
Wiþ alle þe hewes þat him beþ' i-sent.
745 Neuere so feir chaypere
Nedde kyng ne emperere.

Muche more feirschupe⁵ i-non; per was⁵
þer God Almiȝten his in ches;
Þene nis þer such a⁶ Castel non,
750 Ne neuer nas but þulke on⁶,
Ne nener eft after⁷ be ne schal,
For God of henene hit dihte⁸ al,
And wrouȝte⁹ bit hī self and al dude
To alihten in þulke seyre¹⁰ stude.
755 From his kindam¹¹ abone
He cudde¹² þe stude muche loue.

Þis is þe Castel of lone and liase
Of solace, of socour, of joye, and blisse,
Of hope, of bele, of sikernesse,
760 And ful of alle swetnesse.

Þis is þe Mayden [bodi]¹³ so freo:

¹ A. I-tyȝed; II. I-joyned; Fr. simply cocher, i. e. conchés. ² A. beoþ.
³ A. feirschipe. ⁴ There is something wrong here: Fr. has—
Assez plus beante suolt.
⁵ A. and II. a, which V. omits. ⁶ V. and II. on, A. al on. ⁷ A.
after. ⁸ A. made. ⁹ A. wrouhte. ¹⁰ A. feire. ¹¹ A. kyngdom.
¹² A. kudde. ¹³ A. and V. omit this word; II. has 'the maydons body',
and Fr.,   Cent le cors de la pucela.
And compare l. 55. The omission of the genitive termination to *mayden*
is justified by the expression in ll. 55, 959, and several others in this
poem. One or two other instances are—'his fadur blysse' (see note on
l. 585); 'for Marie love', Piers PL Vis., L. 883; 'in Arthur dayes', Romb.
Cl. Morte Arthur, p. 1; 'on launcelot landys', ib. p. 80; 'Gawayne strengthe
gan to in crese', ib. p. 93; 'his souter sone', ib. p. 103; 'the vicounte
lendes', Halliwell's Morte Arthur, p. 265;
And in the *levedy hert* hyt felle
That was the knygbt that ho loved wel,

CASTEL OFF LOUE.

[þer]¹ neuer nas uon² bote heo
þat wiþ so fele³ pewes⁴ i-warned wes,
So⁵ þat swete Mayden⁶ Marie wes.

765 Heo stont In þe mere bi-twene two,
[þat]⁷ heo schilde vs alle from vre fo
þat vs awayteþ day and niht:
Heo vs helpeþ wiþ al hire miht.

Þo roche þat is so trewe and trusti,
770 Þat is þe Maydenes⁸ herte, for-þi
Þat neuer synne þer-wᵗ-inne com,
Acᵗ heo to seruen God al hire nom¹⁰,
And wuste hire wᵗ muche boxūnesse
Hire maidenhod wiþ swetnesse.

775 Þe foundemēt þᵗ faste to þe roche liþ¹¹,
And þe feire greneschipe þer-wiþ,

Seven Sages, l. 2634; 'the emperour sone', lb. l. 3371; 'ln hur fader
pavylon', Emp. Oct. (Hall.), l. 1045; 'to make hys modur pees', lb.
l. 1644;
 I know not an a
 from the wynd-mylne,
 ne a b from a *boke foot*,
Wright's Pol. Poems and Songs, vol. II, p. 57; and of Roberte the Denylle
we are told, p. 8,
 — hys teeth grewe so peryllouslye
 That the noryshe nypples he bote away.
Numerous other examples are such as—helle pyne, helle jates, havene
riche, havene blis, havene riche blisse (Piers Pl. Vis., l. 54), havene
quene, herte bote, herte gleem; expressions which have perhaps a fair
claim to be termed compound nouns.

¹ A. and V. þatı II. has,
 Ther never noon bote hos.
The French is,
 Onkes antre *not* for cele,
i. e. Il n'y *eut* jamais &c.
² A. non.   ³ A. feole.   ⁴ Fr. has,
 Ke de tant *vertus* feust garnie.
⁵ A. as.   ⁶ A. melde.   ⁷ So H.; A. and V. om.   ⁸ A. maidenes.
⁹ A. ak.   ¹⁰ H. alle here hert aboe noma, but the Fr. is—
 Mes a deu seruir se prist.
Compare l. 959.   ¹¹ A. lyþ.

[Þat is]¹ þe Maydenes² bi-leeue³ so riht,
Þat hap al hire bodi i-liht.
For hire bi-leeue⁴, þᵗ is so trewe,
780 Þat euere is grene and euere⁵ newe;
For bi-leeue⁶ is apertement
Of alle vertues⁷ foundement.

Of þe middel henȝ⁸ is to wite
Þe swetnesse and þe feirschipe.
785 Þat is þe bi-tokenyng:
[Þat]⁹ in goode¹⁰ hope, as so ȝong þing,
[Heo]⁹ was so bisy¹¹ in swetnesse
To serueu God in boxumnesse¹².

Þe pridde henȝ and þe on¹³ oncmast,
790 Þat hap oueral his liht i-cast,

¹ So H.: A. and V. om. The French reads thus:
Le fundement auant nome
Cil (de MS.) ka la roche est ferma.
Ki est depaint a color
De se tresbele verdur.
Cest la fol de la uirgine
Ke sun seint quor illumine.
² A. maydens. ³ A. beleeue. ⁴ A. bi-lene. ⁵ A. adds is. ⁶ So
H.: A. and V. read 'hire bi-leeue'. The original translator is hardly
likely to have missed the meaning of words so plain as—
Ker fol est spertement
De intes uertus fondemel;
where the learned bishop doubtless referred not to the Maiden's faith in
particular, but to faith generally, just as Wklif says in the beginning
of his Credo, "It is sooth that bileue is grounde of alle vertues".
⁷ A. vertuwes. ⁸ A. henh. ⁹ These words, which A. and V. omit,
are supplied from H. That they are necessary is evident from the passage itself, and from the French which runs thus:
E puis est la meine color
De si tres bele doncour.
Cest la signefiance
Ke od tendrur en esperance.
Serui tut tens son seignor
En humilite e en doncor.
"And next is the middle colour, of such sweet beauty. This is the
meaning: that with steadfastness (?) in hope she ever served her lord in
humility and gentleness." ¹⁰ A. gode. ¹¹ A. bisi. ¹² A. buxomnesse.
¹³ So V. and H.: A. omits on. See note on L 715.

And as panȝ hit barnde al hit is,
(Nis non of so muche pris;)
Þat is þe clere loue and briht
Þat heo is al wiþ i-liht,
795 And i-tent wiþ þe fair of loue
To serue God þat is hire aboue.

Þe foure smale toures abouten
Þat [witeþ]¹ þe heiȝe tour w⁴-outen,
Foure hed þewes þ' abouts hire i-seoþ,
800 Foure vertues² cardinals³ [þat]⁴ beoþ;

¹ A. and V. wiþ: II.
That krpys the his toure withowtyn.
That II. has preserved the true sense is self-evident. And Fr. has,
Les quatre toreles en haut
Ki gardent la tur danant &c.
Comp. also II. 608 and 825. ² A. vertuwes. ³ I believe I am right in asserting that in Early English an adjective takes a plural termination in *es* only when placed after its noun, as here; and in Early English Poems, p. 43, l. 15, 'þreo *crateres principales*'. Other instances are Chaucer's phrase, which every body knows,
Yet sawgh I hrente the *schippes hoppesteres*,
Knight's Tale. Near the beginning of The Persones Tale we read: 'Many ben the *weyes espirituels* that leden folk to oure Lord Jhesu Christ, and to the regne of glorie'. Further on in the same Tale we read '*thinges espirituelex*'; and in the Tale of Melibæus, '*goodes temporales*' and '*causes materiales*'. In Wright's Political Poems and Songs, vol. II, p. 181, we read——
——the wolle of Englonde
Susteyneth the *comons Ffcmmyngis*, I understonde.
In Maundevile, p. 82, we have: 'and in this Templum Domini weren somtyme *Chanouns Reguleres*'; in p. 125: 'for they have noon Companye, and other many *Causes resonables*'; in p. 181: 'aftre this I have gon toward the *parties meridionales*'; and in p. 92: 'In the Mount Syon weren buryed Kyng David and Kyng Salomon, and many othere *Kynges Jewes* of Jerusalem', where I take the liberty of omitting the comma which the editor puts after *Kynges*, as the phrase seems pretty evidently to mean *Jewish Kings*. But the adjective even after the noun is far more commonly used without this sign of the plural, as 'nonnes Cristene', 'requestes resonable', &c. The only instance that I have noticed in which an adjective used predicatively has the plural in *es* is in Chaucer's Tale of Sir Thopas,
    Of romaunces that ben *reales*,
    Of popes and of cardinales.
⁴ A. and V. þer, II. thei, neither of which can be the true reading, to which l. 827 helps us at once.

¶ þat is, strengþe and sleihschupe¹,
Rihtfulnesse and worschupe²,
Euerichon w' a þat w' ginne,
þat may non vuel³ come þer-inne

805 And whuche heoþ [þe]⁴ preo⁵ hayles ȝet,
þ' w' þe carnels heþ⁶ so wel i-set,
And i-cast w' cūpas and walled aboute,
þat witeþ þe beiȝe tour wiþ-outen?
¶ Bote þe inemaste⁷ bayle, I wot,
810 Bi-tokneþ hire holy maidenhod
þat neuer for no þing i-worsed nas,
So ful of Godes grace heo was.

þe middel hayle, þat wite ȝe
Bi-tokneþ hire holy chastite.
815 And seppen þe [outemaste]⁸ hayle
Bi-tokneþ hire holy sposayle.
Riht me clepeþ hem bayles for-þi,
þat heo hahheþ þis ladi in hire Bayli,
þat hire-self one makeles
820 Is mayden chast and weddet wes.
þorw on of þeos hayles he mot teon,
þat wol on ende i-horwed heon.

þe sone⁹ [berhicans]¹⁰ abouten,
þ' w' gret gin heon i-wrouȝt¹¹ w'-outen

¹ A. sleihschipe.   ² A. worschipe.   ³ A. euel.   ⁴ So B., and the
French ls, 'les trois bailles &c.'   ⁵ A. pre.   ⁶ A. beoþ.   ⁷ Fr.,
 Cele a la plus haut estage.
⁸ A. and V. onemaste; H. otmast. Fr., la foreine baille. Onemaste
could only mean the highest, which would be the innermost. See the
preceding note.   ⁹ A. seuene.   ¹⁰ A. and V. carnels; H. barbacanes.
Compare ll. 695 and 697, and the French—
 E les barbekanes set
 Ki hors des bailles sut fet.
Moreover 'barbicans' really are outworks, as required by the next line;
but 'carnels', Fr. 'kerneaus', are nothing of the sort: see Glossary.
¹¹ A. i-wrouht.

CASTEL OFF LOUE.   39

825 And wiþeþ þis Castel so wel
     Wiþ arwe and wiþ qwarel,
     Þat beþ¹ þe seuen vertues w' winne
     To ouercome þe seuen dedly sinne:
¶   Þat is, pruide, þe biginnynge
830 And þe roote² of al vuel³ þinge⁴,
     Al maat and oner-comen wes
     Þorw boxumnes⁵ þat heo ches;
¶   And hire trewe loue ouercom envye;
     And hire abstinence⁶, glotonye;
835 ¶ And lecherye⁷ heo made fle
     Þorw⁸ hire holy chastite;
¶   And al⁹ was distruyed¹⁰ conetyse
     Þorw hire largesse in vche wyse;
¶   And euere wrappe heo oner-com
840 Þorw mekenesse þat heo nom;
¶   And hire gostliche gladynge
     Destruyed¹¹ sleuþe þorw alle pīge.

     Þe welle springeþ of alle grace
     Þat falleþ þe diches ī vche a place.
845 Godes grace to-deleþ þis
     Þorw meth wiþ-al as his wille is;
     Ac¹² he lonede so þis mayden a-pliȝt¹³,
     Þe folk¹⁴ of grace he hire ȝaf out-riht,
     Þorw¹⁵ whom þe grace þat ouer-fleot
850 Socoureþ al þe world put.
     For-þi me may hire riht clepe and calle,
     "O blessed Ladi ouer opere¹⁶ alle!"

     And what mowe þe dyches be
     But hire polemode pouerte,

---

¹ A. beoþ. For þat beþ = ce sont or das sind compare Ancren Riwle, p. 10: Þat beoð, also he selde, þe god &c. ² A. rote. ³ A. euel. ⁴ As biginnynge is either the nom. or acc. in l. 829, it is clearly impossible that the final e should be sounded; and therefore the final e of þinge must not be pronounced. Comp. ll. 841, 842, where gladynge is a nom. ⁵ A. boxumnes. ⁶ A. abstinence. ⁷ A. lecherie. ⁸ V. þouȝ. ⁹ V. was. ¹⁰ A. distruiȝet. ¹¹ A. distruiȝed. ¹² A. ak. ¹³ A. spliht. ¹⁴ A. folke. ¹⁵ A. þorwh. ¹⁶ A. oþur.

855 Þat nones¹ kūnes assaylyng
Ne may² derne þe tour for no þing;
Þorw whom þe feond is ouer-comon,
And his miht al by-nomen³.

For þis is þe ladi so gent and fre
860 þ' God seide of to þe neddre on þe tre,

¹ A. no. II. changes this line into
    Ther was no mon-kynnes assaylyng,
as l. 875 is metamorphosed into
    That no maner assylyng;
Instead of   þat none kunnes assaylyng.
Our present idiom is 'no kind of assault'; but the literal meaning of the expression in our text is so clear (namely 'assault of no kind'), and this use of *kunnes* so common, that it is strange that the writer of II. should have found it necessary to adopt another phrase. His having done so seems little consistent with the supposition that that text belongs to the early part of the fourteenth century. With the *nones kunnes* before us we may compare
    on aies cunnes wisen
in Laȝ. Br. III, p. 23, (rendered by Sir F. Madden 'in wise of any kind'); *monies kunnes* folc, ib. l, 73; a *rūmes kinnes* wisen, ib. I, 168; on *olches cunnes* wise, ib. I, 344; *anes kunnes* Iweden, ib. III, 207. But more commonly the adjective drops the genitive termination, though this still adheres to the noun; as in the *nane kunnes* of l. 875. With this compare the *fale kunnes* of Laȝ. Br. I, 111, second text; *many kynnes* places, Piers Ploughman's Vision, p. 152; *oþere kynnes* men, ib. p. 177;
    Wel Jarne he him biþoute
    Hou he hire gete monte
    In ani cunnes wise,
MS. Bodl. Digby 86, fol. 165; *alkyns* tren, Halliwell's Morte Arthur, p. 271; *whal kyns* schappe, Rob. of Brunne's Chron., Prol., l. 155. The form *no kynnes* which A. has in the present passage, is found also in Early Engl. Poems, VI. 24, and Judic. p. xiii:
    When thai me smote I stod stilly; agans thaym did I *nokyns* grefe.
But not infrequently the noun also dropped the case-termination, and accordingly we find *feole kune* in Laȝ. Br., i, p. 111, first text; *wyth alle kyn* welthe, Emp. Oct. (Hall.), l. 200; as also,
    We love the Lord in *alkyn* thyng, Jud. p. xx;
and in Towneley Myst. p. 33,
    With the ahal no man fyght, nor do the *no kyn* wrake.
Other forms are *moni kunne*, *allirkin*, *this kin*, *what kin*.
² A. mai.   ³ A. bi-nomen.

CASTEL OFF LOUE.   41

       þ' per scholde come a woman [blyuo]¹,
       þat scholde al his pouste² to-dryuo³.
       I-blessed beo þis buyrde⁴ of pryz⁵,
       þat oner al opere i-blessed is;
  865 þat so feir was and good so sone⁶
       þat of hir bodi⁷ God made his trone
       To his owne⁸ gistenynge,
       And nom flesch and blood⁹ of hire, to brige
       His folk out of prisoū:
  870 þat was vre garysoun¹⁰.

       þis ladi is feir and good and fre¹¹,
       Whon heo¹² hap so muche boūte,
       More þen eny schaft þat wos;
       For-þi þe rihtwys sone¹³ hire ches,
  875 And schadewede on hire in wolde¹⁴,
       And feirede hir¹⁵ more a pousend folde.

¹ So H., and so the rhyme demands: A. and V. blipe. There is no
corresponding word in Fr. ² Here H. in reading hed is nearer to the
French, which is,
                    Kone femme venderoit
                    Ke tut son chief quasseroit.
³ A. to-drius. ⁴ A. buirde. ⁵ A. pris. ⁶ A. soone. ⁷ H. soule.
⁸ A. onne. ⁹ A. blod. ¹⁰ A. garisoun. ¹¹ A. omits and fre. ¹² A.
he. ¹³ H., the sonne of ryhtwesnes, which agrees better with the
French:
                    Mels quant li solans de droiture.
                    Dens son seint cors enombrat
                    Mil ltant embeli lad.
¹⁴ This wolde (which = power) H. turns into the auxiliary verb:
                    And on heere when he shadowe wolde,
as Mandevile (Prol.) writes: 'and there he wolde of his blessednesse
encombre him in the seyd blessed and glorious Virgine Marie.' It
seems however as if the original translator, whose words the writer of
H. misunderstood and forsook, has in this instance rightly recognized the
bishop's scriptural allusion in enumbrat (see preceding note), and, to
complete his rhyme, had recourse to the gospel narrative to help him
out. The words of St. Luke in Jerome's version are: 'Et respondens
angelus dixit ei, Spiritus sanctus superveniet in te, et virtus altissimi
obumbrabit (= Grk. ἐπισκιάσει) tibi; ideoque et quod nascetur sanctum
vocabitur filius dei' (Lu. 1, 35). ¹⁵ A. hire.

Þorw¹ þe faste þat be con in teo,
And at þe out-þong he letta faste beo².
How³ so þat was, beo we stille,
880 For of alle þing God may don his willa.

A derworþe qween⁴ I so get and fre,
Þat helpeþ alle þat fleoþ to þe,
Mi soule is come to þe for nede⁵,
Þat at þi gate bat and loude doþ grede;
885 Bat and gredeþ and loude gon crye⁶,
"Help me swete Mayden⁷ Marie:
Vndo, Ladi; I þe bi-seche
Þou let me a luitel cleche
Of pulke [grace]⁸ þat alle fronere,
890 Þat gostliche beoþ in herte pouere⁹.

"Lo hou I am bi-set heer-oute
Wiþ my þreo fon¹⁰ al aboute;
¶ Þe fend¹¹ þ' wiþ me fihteþ euere,
¶ Þe world, my flesch, heo ne stinteþ neuere;

¹ V. þon), corrected by a later hand which inserted r. ² Compare
Ancren Riwle, p. 38—'Þet ilke blissfule bearn iboren of þine clene bodie
to moncunne bele wiðuten euerich bruche, mid ihol meidenhod, &c.' The
words in italic are correctly rendered by Mr. Morton in his note, 'sine
omni raptura'. ³ A. hon. ⁴ A. qwen. ⁵ A. neode. ⁶ A. crije.
⁷ A. malden. ⁸ So II., though A. and V. omit this word. The French
of this passage runs thus:
            Franche pucele raine
            De reful forte fermine.
            A toi est malme [sic MS.] venue
            Ki a ta porte huche e hue.
            Hue huche. e hue e crie
            Duce dame. aie. aie.
            Raine dame oures oures
            Vn pol reposer me lasser.
            De la *grace* que garit
            Les poures en esperit.
⁹ 'Beati pauperes spiritu', Matt. 5, 3 (Vulg.). ¹⁰ A. foon. In the Tale
of Melibæus also we have mention of the 'thre enemyes of mankynde,
that is to say, thy flessche, the feend, and the world'; and in Ancren
Riwle, p. 106. ¹¹ A. feond.

895 Wiþ-outen eny meþ on me heo foþ¹,
    Swiþe gret harm heo me doþ.
    Gret parlemēt heo habbeþ i-nome².

    "Þe fend³ furst is forþ i-come²;
    "Wiþ þreo hostes he deþ⁴ me gret wo—
900 Wiþ pruide, and wrappe, and sleuþe also.
¶ Þe world me haþ wᵗ two hostes bistōde;
    Þat is wiþ conetyse and onde⁵.
    And my flesch me fondeþ to spille
    Wᵗ glotenye⁶ and wiþ vuel⁷ wille.
905 ¶ Gret wrappe¹ heo habbeþ to me i-nome:
    I am as campion⁹ ouer-come.
    But þou me helpe, mayde Marie,
    Ichabbe¹⁰ i-lore þe maystrie¹¹.
    [Þow þat art to alle febulle leche,
    Þow let me of þy dyches cleche,]¹²
    Þer¹³ þe castel is faste and stable
910 And Charite is constable."

    Of þis castel Ichabbe a luitel told,
    Ac more me miȝte¹⁴ a þousend fold;
    For alle þe godschupes þᵗ ī þe world is,
    Out of þis Castel i-comen is.
915 ¶ Þorw þis laddre God heuene-[drihte]¹⁵
    From heuene in-to eorþe alihte,

---

¹ A. foth. ² These two lines are transposed in A. ³ A. feond.
⁴ A. doþ. ⁵ H. gives this line thus:
            That is with covetyse and hate he wold me fond.
See Gloss., s. v. onde. ⁶ A. glotonye. ⁷ A. euel. ⁸ A. wappe. ⁹ A. camploun. ¹⁰ A. Ich habbe. ¹¹ A. maistrie. ¹² So H., these two lines being omitted by A. and V. The French is—
            Si la grace ne maie
            Tost aurai perdu la mestrie.
        815 Tu que fiebles redrescez
            Fai me poser au fossez.
            Ou li chastel est estable
            E charite rest constable.
¹³ A. þer þer þe castel &c. ¹⁴ A. mihte. ¹⁵ A. and V. dihte: H., as in a multitude of other passages, modernizes into *God Allmyȝht*.

And nom of hire his monhede
þorw whom he wrey¹ his Godhede.

Þis is þe ȝard² þat bereþ þe flour,
920 Þat maiden þat bar hire creatour.
And þus þe child is i-boren³ to vs,
And such a sone i-ȝene to vs.

And nis he wonderful þer-fore
Whon he is þus for vs i-bore?
925 So muche wonder nis of no þinge,
As two kuynden to-geder bringe⁴,
And þat eiþer kuynde wiþ-alle
Habbe þat wole to heom⁵ bi-falle,
Þat neuer nouþer ne woute no wiht,
930 Ac þat eiþer habbe al his riht.

Þat is Jhū Godes⁶ sone,
Þ' fro heuene to eorþe wolde come
To sauȝte⁷ his sustren þ' were⁶ to-boren,
And dilyueren⁹ þe prison þ' was forloren.
935 Two kuynden he haþ, we wite bi þon,
Þat he is soþ God and soþ mon¹⁰.

Bi-hold now mon to Godes miht,
And his deden hou heo beoþ diht;
Þ' þª a-boute nouȝt¹¹ fer se,
940 Ac¹² hi-hold hou boxum he wolde be
Þat he wolde be¹³ boren of womon
And for vre sake bi-comen mon.
And seþþen be-hold hou he vs redeþ,
And in-to sauete vs ledeþ,

---

¹ A. wreyþ; H. kend.   ² Compare Wiclif's rendering of Hebr. 9. 4, 'the ȝerde of aaron that florischid'.   ³ A. boren, without i-.   ⁴ A. bryngþ. "To-geder bringe" here and in l. 990 for "to-geder to bringe". For the to omitted where another to almost immediately precedes, see Gloss., s. v. To. H. gives "in oon to bryng".   ⁵ A. hem.   ⁶ A. Goddes.   ⁷ A. sauhten.   ⁸ A. weore.   ⁹ A. deliuren.   ¹⁰ The translator has here omitted 68 lines of the French.   ¹¹ A. nouht.   ¹² A. ah.   ¹³ A. beo.

945 On ful swete manere and on non oþur.
And seiþ þus to vs: "Leue broþur[1],
I seo[2] þe mis-lyken and al for-jemed[3],
And out of þin owne[4] lond i-flemed[5];
And þou seost wel þat for no þing
950 þow[6] hast of þi self no keueryng.

¶ Ne beo þou in wonhope non,
Ac[7] ful siker þou beo per-on;
Ȝif þ[8] wole me loue and vnderstode[9],
I chul þe bringe in-to þin owne[9] londe.
955 ¶ Ententyfliche[10] þou herken[11] to me,
And do þat ich[12] comaude þe[13].

"Mi jok is softe i-nowh[14] to weren,
And my burþene[15] liȝt[16] i-nouh to beren.
To Merci bi-houe I am al i-nome,
960 And þus I am for þe i-come;
And Ich[15] þe rede þou suwe me:
I chulle[17] þe batayle nyme for þe.
¶ To ple I chulle þis princes[18] hauen,

[1] A. broþer. [2] A. se. [3] A. for-jemet. [4] A. onne. [5] A. i-flemet.
[6] A. þou. [7] A. ak. [8] A. vnderstonde. [9] A. oune. [10] A. ententi-
fliche. [11] A. herkne. [12] A. I bis. [13] The French of this passage,
which is very inaccurately printed in the Caxton Society's edition, is as
follows:

   E si nous dit beaudos frere.
   Jo te noi ci esgares
   De ton pais eissiles.
 925 E al ueez apertement
   Ke par toi nas recouremël.
   Ne solez ia en desperance
   Ne de co naies dotance.
   Ke al crerre me nolltes
 930 Ton heritage tot aures.
   Oes mei tut anlement
   E feies mon comandement.

[14] A. i-nouh. [15] A. burþen. [16] A. liht. [17] A. chul. [18] 'This
princess' is doubtless Mercy; but the translator has here quite misread
or misunderstood the original, which is,
   Princes por toi voil pleider
 940 E ton droit noil chalanger.

"And þi rihte I chulle cranen;
965 For Icham¹ of þi lynage:
I may cranen þin heritage.
¶ And Icham¹ of freo nacion:
Me onȝte² i-here my reson.
And Ichabbe i-wust w¹ wynne³
970 Þe þreo lawen w¹-outen synne.
¶ For þe I chulle to⁴ batayle wende,
[And]⁵ siker beo þⁿ of ful good ende,
For I chulle an ende ouercome þ¹ fiht,
And to-dreynen al þi riht.
975 Ne darstou on erþe⁶ þechen⁷ elles nouht⁸,
But God and þī enecriete⁹ to loue ī trewe
pouȝt."

Lord, wiuch¹⁰ freschipe¹¹! hose nome ȝeme;
Who he þ¹ welde¹² al þig and al mai deme,
Vs schewed¹³ such freschip¹¹ and swetnes,
980 And a forbysne of boxumnes¹⁴.
Ac þulke forbisne¹⁵ me luitel telleþ to,
And selden I þe world i-seȝe ne ȝore haþ do¹⁶.

¹ A. *I am* (with an erasure after the *I*) *bis*. ² V. outs. ³ A. winne.
⁴ A. þe. ⁵ So H.: A. and V. for. In Fr. there is no conjunction:
Pur toi prendrai la bataille
Saneres bone definaille.
⁶ A. corþe. ⁷ A. þeken. ⁸ A. nouȝt. ⁹ A. enen cristne. ¹⁰ A.
whuch. ¹¹ A. fredschip *bis*. ¹² A. walde. ¹³ Other uncontracted weak
preterites in which the final -*e* is dropped will be found in ll. 1266 (V.),
1270, and 1388. See Gloss. s. v. *And-last*. ¹⁴ A. boxunnes. ¹⁵ A.
forbysne: H. reads—
And thuke bysenes me lytull tellit to,
And sylden in the world this verin is do.
The French of this passage stands thus in the MS.:
Deu. quen docur quen franchise
Kant cil hi unte rien lustise.
Tant nus mustrad amistez
E ensample de humilitez.
965 Mes cele ensamp est poi tenue
E trop reument el mund venue.
¹⁶ So A. and V., but at least as to the number of syllables H. has
the best reading in this line.

CASTEL OFF LOUE. 47

For þe worldlich¹ mon euere i-liche
Loueþ þīg þat is worldliche,
985 ¶ Ac þe gost of charite and of þolemodnesse²
Loueþ euer goodschipe³ and boxomnesse⁴.
¶ For whon to þe world hī ɪeueþ⁵ þe mon,
And þe worldes good hī waxeþ on,
He ne þēkeþ on God, ne nō oþer þynge⁶
990 Bote worldes catel to-geder bringe⁷.
¶ And whō þe catel haþ þe maystrie⁸ alas!,
[Hit]⁹ is in his cofre bi-loke so fast,
Þat al he bi-comeþ onergart proud,
And mis-doþ his neiʒebors boþe stille¹⁰ and
loud¹¹.

995 No þing ne wilneþ he largesse,
But lordschupe and beiʒnesse;
Þe forbysne¹² of boxnnesse¹³ i-wys¹⁴
Al þorw pruyde¹⁵ forʒeten is.
¶ Þeose ne mowen Jhc̄ suwen wiþ,
1000 For heore dede al to-lyth¹⁶,
Ne his red ne leeueþ heo nouʒt.
Whi þēne woldē heo wilnen ouʒt

¹ So A. and V., while H. is for once more accurate and appends the final e—*worldyche.* ² A. polmodnes. ³ A. godschipe. ⁴ A. boxūnes.
⁵ A. ɪineþ. ⁶ A. oþur þige. ⁷ See note on l. 920. ⁸ A. malstrie.
⁹ H. hit, A. and V. þt hit. ¹⁰ A. stil. ¹¹ The French of these four lines is—

Kant auoir ad la mestrie
Si ferm ens ses las le lie.
Kil deuient fier e orgoillos
E a ses neisins surfeitus.

That is to say—"quand la richesse a la prééminence, elle le lie si fermement dans ses lacs, qu'il devient &c." The second of these lines our translator has evidently not understood, and his rendering is both inexact and in our MSS. ungrammatical. H. reads thus:

And when worldly godys han the mastri,
Hit maketh mon so rebell and hye,
That he waxeth wonder prowde, &c.

¹² H. verīn. ¹³ A. buxomnes. ¹⁴ A. I-wis. ¹⁵ A. pruīde. ¹⁶ So A. and V., not þȳ: compare ll. 491, 895, and 1043.

Of heritage in his kyndom¹,
Þanj he in batayle þe ple bi-won,
1005 Whon heo doþ al þ' he for-bat²,
And no þig doþ of þat he hat,
Ac euer sochoþ pride and heijnesse,
Ne biddeþ³ heo nouȝt of boxunesse?⁴

For-þi⁵ Lucifer, as ȝe habbeþ herd telle,
1010 Fel frō heuene a-doun to helle;
And also I drede heo scholdē an ende,
Þulke þat suche werkes doþ, after hī wende⁶.
Ac⁷ 1 ne sigge hit not for⁸ þon
Þat mai⁹ ful wel eueriche goodamon¹⁰

¹ A. kindom. ² A. for-bad, but the present tense is evidently correct: see Fr. quoted below. ³ A. kepeþ; H. loveth: see below. ⁴ With these ten lines let us compare first the French original, and then the reading of H.

Icons therum ne alwent mis
Kar lur fet les contralis.
875 Son conseill ne voillent crere
E coment donca par quel affera.
Voillent cil riens demander
Ne del heritage den aueir.
Kant il[s] funt quankil defent
960 E despisent co kil aprent.
Ne voillent rien dumiliance
Mes reuilen la den pussance.

And now H., pp. 43, 44.

Thes synnes mow not Crist sue,
For thei beth of evyll vertue:
And whos his vertu levyth nowght,
Why shuld he wyllen owght
Of his eritage in his kyndome,
That he thorgh plee and bataylle wone;
And ever aȝeynst his byddyng well do,
And aȝeyns here soulys allso;
And ever secheth prude and hienesse,
And loveth nothyng bucsomnesse.

⁵ A. þerfore. ⁶ Here H. inserts—
But ȝef thei bem amende
Of that that they dude God afende.

⁷ A. ak. ⁸ See Glossary. ⁹ A. may. ¹⁰ A. god mon.

CASTEL OFF LOUE. 49

1015 Habbe gret lordschupe¹ and heijnesse,
Castels, and toures, and gret richesse,
And may²[wel don]³ and Godes wille holde,
And libbe God to queme wel ȝif he wolde;
¶ ȝif he lyueþ⁴ ī [lone]⁵ and ī bonunesse⁶,
1020 In sopschupe and in rihtwysnes.
For God wilneþ no þíg on eorþe her⁷,
But al mōnes herte w⁸ trewe loue and cler.

Nou⁹ mihte⁹ sū mon aaken pus:
Hou wolde God plede for vs?
1025 Hou¹⁰ he eny batayle nom,
And won vre riȝte¹¹ and a fend ouer-com?
Lnstneþ penne to me son,
And I chulle ow tellen hou.
Þo Jhesu Godes sone in þe world was i-bore,
1030 So stille and derne he was þe fend fore,
Þat he of his come riht nouȝt nuste,
[Ac]¹² to ben lord and eyre þit enere he truste,
As he hedde ben, ac his miht was bi-nome,
Þo þ¹ Jhesu was i-bore and ī-to þ¹ world
i-come.
1035 Wel þe fend hī seiȝ¹³ in mōnes weeden,
Ac he nuste¹⁴ what he was, ne wynch were
his dede.
He hī seiȝ¹⁵ wel mon, and¹⁶ i-come of
mōkune,
Ac¹⁷ enere ī þe world he liuede wiþ-oute
sine¹⁸.

---

¹ A. lordschipe.   ² A. mai.   ³ A. and V. walden; H.,
And may ȝet Goddis wylle don and holde.
⁴ A. limeth.   ⁵ A. and V. londe; H. and Fr. charite.   ⁶ A. bonumnes.
⁷ A. heer.   ⁸ H. how.   ⁹ A. miȝte.   ¹⁰ A. how.   ¹¹ A. rihte.   ¹² A.
and V. as; H. but: Fr. has, Mels quidoni par tot seignnriz, 1. e. mals ll
prätendait dominer partout.   ¹³ A. seih.   ¹⁴ V. nnst.   ¹⁵ A. he selȝ hi.
¹⁶ A. omits and.   ¹⁷ A. ak.   ¹⁸ A. synne.

d

CASTEL OFF LOUE.

þe fend wondrede swiþe, and seide, "What
                      arton?
1040 Wher þ[u] beo Godes sone þ[1] art i-comen' non?
Al þis wyde world I chul jenen[2] þe,
So þat þou bouwe[3] and honoure me."

RESPONDIT JESUS.

Þo seide Jhesu[4], "Go awei[5], Sathan[6], go:
Þi kuynde lord ne schalt þow' fonde so[a]."

DIABOLUS DICIT.

1045 ¶ "What wenestou? I ne mowe vnderstonde,
Þat Icham[7] prince and lord of þis londe"[8],

---

[1] A. I-come.   [2] A. jeue.   [3] A. bowe.   [4] A. Jhē.   [5] A. wel.
[6] The MSS. keep the Latin and French &c. here. So in MS. Harl. 2253,
Fo. 55b. we have—

    Alle herknep to me non
    a strif wolle y tellen on.
    of þhū sut of sathan
    þo iþū was to helle ygan. &c.

On the other hand Wicliffe writes: 'And Poule be-toke þe fornicari to
saþanas till a tyme, þat his spirit schulde be sane.' (Apology for the
Lollards, Camden Society's edition, p. 24.) Elsewhere Wicliffe names
Barthelmew, Hector Thebanus, Athenis, and on p. 54, Sathanas: on p. 31,
Thimoþe. In the Early English Poems (ed. Furnivall) we read, p. 31,
þer is þe loþe sathanas. & belsebuc þe ealde.
Whether the th. was kept in the MSS. of poems often cannot be determined from the printed editions, the þ of the MSS. being everywhere,
by some editors, turned into th. Of the word now before us, Satan was
one form, as in Cædmon and Robert de Brunne, and another was Satanas
(the only Greek form), as in Tat., Bede, the Ormulum, and the Harrowing of Hell (MS. Bodl. Digby 86, fo. 119 sqq.).   [7] A. schaltou.
[a] H. strangely alters this line:
    I am thy Lord, thou shalt fynde me so!
   [8] A. þ. I. am (sic).   [10] I understand this passage thus: 'What
meanest thou? I cannot be a subject, who am prince and lord &c.' See
Gloss. a. voce. Understand and þat. H. turns these lines into—
    What thenketh the? mayst thou not understond?
    Seyde the fynde, I am Lord &c.
The French is:

CASTEL OFF LOUE. 51

And in þe selsyue habbe longe i-be
þorw þe heiȝe kyng þat graūt hit me.
Alle þing I seo, and alle þīg Ich wot;
1050 Hut one þi pouȝt no þing I not.
þou nymest¹ ful muche an hond,
To be-nymen² me eny þing in þis lond.
þauȝ³ I nabbe miht ouer þe,
Weneastou my preye to be-nyme⁴ me?
1055 Nay⁵, for þat foreward⁶, þorw Sop and Riht,
Faste ī Godes court is congraffet a-pliht;
Þat hose passede Godes beste⁷,
He scholde⁸ be⁹ myn, and in sūne¹⁰ leste
An ende dyen þorw hard deþ i-nouh:
1060 And þe kyng of heoene nul¹¹ do no wouh.
What weneatou such foreward⁸ breke,
Þat was in Godes court i-speke?"

RESPONDIT JHC.

And þo swete Jhesu hī onswerde and tolde,
"Þat foreward⁸ on ende wel was i-holde¹²;
1065 Ac þ" hit bi-gonne formast to breke,
Þo þ" þorw treson¹³ to monkuynde¹⁴ speke,

E lhesu dist as anthasus
Tou seignor deu ne tēpteras.
E cil dist donc ke neu tu fere
1030 Prince sul de ceste terre.

¹ A. mymest. ² A. binime. ³ A. þauh. ⁴ A. bi-nyme. ⁵ A.
nal. ⁶ A. forward ter. ⁷ V. repeats—of course simply per aphaima—
Hose passede Godes heste.
⁸ A. scholde. ⁹ A. beo. ¹⁰ A. synne. ¹¹ A. nil. ¹² A. God wol
wel holde. II. makes sad havoc of this passage;
And tho swete Jhesu him ouswered and tolde,
And seyde that foreward myȝht not be holde;
Thow thiself formest dedest hit brake &c.
The French is: Lors respondi li dux ihesu
Li couenant fu bien tenu.
Mels tu primes lenfreinsistes
1040 Kant en traison al serf dsistes.
Tu ne murras &c.
¹³ A. tresun. ¹⁴ A. monkynde.

d 2

And seidest þ[1] treo hi was forbode
Lest[1] he bedde þe miht of Gode;
Ac[1] wolde he of þe appel ete,
1070 Þenne þ[n] seidest he bedde i-gete[1],
For he scholde konen al þ[1] God con,
And he scholde neuer dio[4] for þon.
He a-gulte þorw þe, and elles he wer[5]skere.
Vnderstond[6] my reson[7], þif hit skile were
1075 [Þat][8] þou heddest alle forward of me
And þ[u] noldest bolde he as a-nont þe."

DIABOLUS DICIT.

"Al Ich am bi-trayȝed[9]," qd þe fend þo,
"Non Ich am þorw ple oner-come so.
Of whom and hon comeþ hit,
1080 Such reson[10] and such wit,
Þat þou so baldeliche darst nyman þe
Forte dispute[11] a-ȝeynes me?
Þorw ple Ichabbe i-loren al anon;
[Ac][12] so ne may[13] hit nonȝt gon.
1085 Algate he haþ mis-don,
Þorw[14] whom he is in my prison;
And bote he beo for-bouȝt of me,
He ne ouȝte[15] from wo disseysed[16] be."

[1] A. leste.   [1] A. ak.   [2] That is, 'he would have gained' = 'he would be the gainer by it'. But I suspect the true reading is, 'he schulde i-gete', the i-gete being an infinitive = A.S. begítan, but mistaken by the copyist for a participle.   [4] A. dye.   [5] A. were.   [6] A. voderstond.   [7] A. reson.   [8] So H.: A. þauh, V. þauȝ; but this conjunction seems quite out of place. The meaning evidently is: 'Listen to reason, whether it would be just that thou shouldst receive (the fulfilment of) all the conditions from me, and yet thou shouldst not choose to abide by them as against thyself.' Fr. does not help much: it is as follows:

    Ore esgardez donc reison,
1045 Vens tu de couenant loir
    Kant conenant ne uens tenir?

[9] A. bi-trayet.   [10] A. reson.   [11] A. dispute.   [12] A. and V. and, H. bot, Fr. mes.   [13] A. mal.   [14] A. þor.   [15] A. ouhte.   [16] A. disceysed.

RESPONDIT JESUS.

Þo swete Jhesu to him con sugge,
1090 "And Ichulle hi' þenne for-bugge."
¶ "3if þou wolt him bugge to his feore,
He schal costen þe ful deore."

"Hou¹ deore?" quaþ Jhesu þo.
"As he is worþ, er þenne he go
1095 Out of bonde of my prison²."
¶ "Þat is skile," quaþ Jhesu, "and good reson³;
Ne kep I nou3t⁴ to-peynes riht
þorw maystrie⁵ bi-nyme þe no wiht."

DIABOLUS DICIT.

¶ "No, ac er⁶ he dilyuered be,
1100 Þou most al so⁷ muche delyuere me
As al þis world is [worþ]⁸ atte frome,
Wiþ alle pulke þ' scholen herafter come."

JHC DIXIT.

"Blepeliche," qd Jhc̄, "al I chul⁹ don þis,
For my luttel¹⁰ fynger more worþ is

¹ A. how.   ² A. prisonn.   ³ A. resoun.   ⁴ A. nouht.   ⁵ A. maistrie.
⁶ A. ar.   ⁷ For *al so* A. and H. have *as*.   ⁸ So H.; A. and V. have *nou*. The French of this passage, which in the printed poem is disfigured by two or three misprints, runs thus:
1065   E dist li dos Jhesu benoit
       Co est bien reison e droit.
Fo. 72.   Contre droit ne noll io mie
       Tolir toi riens par maestrie.
       Fai le me donc. volentiers
1070   Kert co donc ke tu quiers?
       Io te dirai bien san faille
       Rendez moi donc que tant vaille.
       Com fol ore tns cil del mond
       E quanhs pres tns lors uendront.
1075   Voleutiers dist li tut cest frai
       Kar mieus naut mo petit del. &c.
⁹ A. ichulle.   ¹⁰ A. leste.

54   CASTEL OFF LOUE.

1105 þen such an hondred¹ worldes ben,
      W¹ al þat folk þ¹ me may herafter sen².''

              DIABOLUS DICIT.

      ¶ þe fend³ þo to Jhesu onswere con:
      "Þat is al sop, I seo bi þon.
      For þᵘ maiȝt al þe world demen and dihte:
1110 For nou ouer þe nabbe I no miȝte.
      And woldestou þi finger ȝeue⁴, þauȝ⁵ þᵘ so
                                        ongge,
      So voworþ and so vyl⁶ chaffare to bugge?''

              RESPONDIT JESUS.

      "Ȝe, and al my bodi for his rannsoun,
      But I ebul⁷ hi habbe ont of prisonn.''
1115 ¶ "Þou most ȝit more do, ar þᵘ him habbe so:
      Þolen on eorþe wandreþe and wo;
      And ȝif þou wole a-menden his wouȝ⁸,
      Þou most deþ þolen þorw strōg pyne i-nonȝ.''

      And þo swete Jhesu hī onswerde þo:
1120 "Al þat⁹ þon hast seid, al schal be do;
      For Soþ seide hit onȝts ben so,
      And Riht com after (and ȝef)¹⁰ þe dom þo;
      And more þē þᵘ hast i-seid I chulle don
      To diliuere¹¹ þe pral ont of prison.''

1125 ¶ Þo was þe fend siker, and wende wel eþe
      Forte haue bi-ȝeten þorw his deþe;
      ¶ Ac¹² he was cauȝt and oner-comen,
      As flsch þat is w¹ hok i-nomen,

---

¹ A. hundret.   ² A. seon.   ³ A. feond.   ⁴ A. ȝiue.   ⁵ A. þau.
⁶ A. vil.   ⁷ A. chulle.   ⁸ A. wouh.   ⁹ V. adds a second þat.   ¹⁰ So
II., these words being omitted by A. and V. The French, as well as
the evident meaning of the passage, shows that the verb is necessary:
          Kar uerite le deulss
          E puls lad luge iustise.
¹¹ A. delynere.   ¹² A. ah, II. and.

CASTEL OFF LOUE.

      þat whon þe worm he swoleweþ a-last¹,
1130 He is bi þe hok I-tiȝed² fast.

      A! Mon, nim³ ȝeme and vnderstond⁴ þe
      Hou synliche I herte God loueþ þe,
      Þ' wolde deþ poli͡e, þorw pyne⁵ w'-oute meþ,
      To sane þi soule fro pyne of deþ.
1135 Al vre gult on hī he wolde take,
      And lodliche was bi-lad al for vre sake.
      For he þat neuer no sūne⁶ dude,
      Ne neuer nas w' fulþe i-founden I no stude,
      In alle⁷ þe lymes þat hap þe mon
1140 Seppe⁸ Adam formest sunne bi-gon,
      Wolde þ' his lymes alle i-pyned were,
      To maken vs of sūne al quit and skere.
      For vre vnwrestschupe⁹ here
      Þe corowne of þornes on his hed he beere¹⁰;
1145 And for vre folye also
      His eȝen¹¹ weore blynt-wharnet¹² bo;
      And al was his face bi-foulet w' spot,
      And eke grete boffetes¹³ amōg me hī smot;
¶ And for vre speche vnwreste and vyl
1150 Atter heo hī dude to drīke i-meynt¹⁴ w' eisil¹⁵.

      Þe otewyse werkes as þere anonden¹⁶

---

¹ H. the worme swolewe that the last.   ² A. i-tyȝed.   ³ A. nym.
⁴ A. vnderstond.   ⁵ A. pine.   ⁶ A. synne.   ⁷ A. al.   ⁸ Fr. gives a
much better sense—

      Dont Adam primes pechad.

⁹ A. vnwresteschipe.   ¹⁰ A. bere.   ¹¹ A. eȝen.   ¹² A. blintwharued,
H. blynwherved.   ¹³ A. buffetes.   ¹⁴ A. i-meyn.   ¹⁵ A. eisyl.   ¹⁶ So
the line stands in the MSS., but it is evidently corrupt. H. gives this
distich thus:

      For unlawfull werk us avonde,
      He was peersed thorgh foot and honde.

Which must be rendered: "For countless misdeeds he was pierced &c.",
for the *avonde* admits no other explanation that I can see but that which
would connect it with the Lat. *abundare* and the Romance *habundos,
avondos, aondos, aundos* (see Raynouard, s. v. *onda*). But the passage

He lette bope purlen his feet¹ and hoden;
And for vre woke ponjtes he polede smerte,
þ' me his syde purlede rijt² to þe herte.
1155 ¶ What miht³ he þene do for vs more?
No tonge may tellen of þat sore⁴
Ne no mōnes herte ne mihte⁵ þenche⁶ so,
As he polede for vs pyne and wo.

And ho is þat ne mijte⁷ habbe pite
1160 Of such frendschupe⁸ and charite?
Such beo þe dunies of batayle
Þat he polede for vs wiþ-outen⁹ fayle.
Ac¹⁰ he polede to deþe¹¹ ben i-brouȝt:
Vre deþ þorw his deþ he haþ for-bouȝt.

1165 For more polede he an¹² hondret folde
Serwe and pyne, þo he dyen¹³ wolde,
Þen þe fend mihte¹⁴ for eny synne¹⁵
Leggen hond¹⁶ vppon monkunne.

thus read would imply that Christ was pierced for *his own* misdeeds in-
numerable, which is just what Fr. contradicts:

E pur nos manois *les forcins*
Se lessa percer plas e meins.
Pur nostre manois penser &c.

(Sic MS.: Mr. Cooke prints *forcins* and *postre*.) Translate: "And for our
evil deeds which were *not his own* he allowed &c." As to 'anonde' for
anonden, the *n* is very distinct in the MSS., and if this were the Romance
word, the final -*en* could not be accounted for. I suspect the line ought
to begin with the preposition *for*, and that 'as þere anonden' (or perhaps
'as pere anonden', see note on l. 1401) ought to mean 'as there imputed
to him', or 'which were not his own', or 'which we were guilty of'.
Compare—

Al þat god suffrid of pine, hit nas noȝt for *is owen* gilt;
Ok hit was man for sin pine: þat wer for sin in helle ipilt.
Fall and Passion, l. 7, Furnivall's Early English Poems, p. 13.

¹ A. fel. ² A. riht. ³ A. myht. ⁴ So A. and V.; H. has 'telle
of his score'. ⁵ A. mijte. ⁶ A. þechen. ⁷ A. mihte. ⁸ A. frend-
schipe. ⁹ A. wt onte. ¹⁰ A. ah, H. and. ¹¹ A. deþ. ¹² A. and.
¹³ A. dijen. ¹⁴ A. mijte. ¹⁵ A. sunne. ¹⁶ This *hond* seems much

CASTEL OFF LOUE.

For þe soule loueþ þe bodi so,
1170 þat neuere heo nole hi wende fro
For no pyne, ne for sore,
þauȝ me hit to-hewe euermore,
Er þe fyf wittes ben loren out-riȝt,
Al heore vertue and al heore miȝt[1].

1175 þat is þe siht, and þe herynge,
þe speche, and þe smellynge,
And þe felynge, he schal leosen an[2] ende,
Ar he wole from[3] þe bodi wende[4].
Kuynde ne may for no þinge
1180 þole her þe tipelynge.

Ac[5] he þat alle þing mai[6] wolde
Doublede his peyne an hondred[7] felde;
For þo he pynede on þe Crois
He ȝaf his soule wiþ loud voys.
1185 þer he schewede þ[t] he was God so:
Vre Ransoum[8] he dude þo.
þe bodi[9] ȝit[9] linede wiþ-oute fayle,
And so he ouercom þe batayle.
Kuynde ne mihte þole such peyne non,
1190 For þe feend ne miȝte hit nener legen[10] on.

And Marie, Mayden schene,
Mihtful Moder and milde Qwene,
For deol mongen I ne may
þe pyne þ[t] þ[u] þoledest þulke day.
1195 Ac þe prophecye of Symeon
Was folfuld[11] þo bi þon;
As wiþ sword in þulke stounde
þon heddest þo ful bitter woūde;

In the way: H. omits it. The French is—
Ke diables neurent poeir
A humeine nature charger.
[1] A. miht. [2] A. and. [3] A. fro. [4] A. weende. [5] A. ak, H. but. [6] A. may.
[7] A. hūdred. [8] A. raunson. [9] Illegible in A. [10] A. legge. [11] A. fulfuld.

CASTEL OFF LOUE.

      Ac[1] þi joye doublede an hondrut[2] folde,
1200 Þo he from dep vp-rysen wolde.
  ¶ For nouȝt worþ[3] weore[4] his passion,
      Neore his resurexion[5].
      Þou[6] seye openliche in alle þinge
      Of his batayle þe endynge,
1205 Þorw whom þe fend was al mat[7],
      And þe world for-bouȝt and brouȝt in stat.
      Þe troupe of vs, and þe beleene[8] also,
      Bi-leuede[9] al in þe þo.

      In wonhope weore his disciples vchon,
1210 Ac[10] þou weore stndefast euer in on;
      Ne miȝte[11] þe no þig tornen out,
      In trewe bileue euere þ[12] weore[13], stille and
                                 loud.
      Marie, Mooder[13] of pite,
      Mayden[14] ful of alle bonte,
1215 Vre bi-leene was þo in þe i-wis;
      And nou[15] al vre hope is
      Þat þou[16] bi-seche þi sone for vs,
      Þat so on rode for-bouȝt[17] vs.

      Ȝe habbeþ i-herd of swete Jhesu,
1220 Hou[18] he þorw his muchel vertu
      Vs redeþ to goode[19] euer-more,
      And hou[19] he wolde vs plede fore,
      And hou[19] he wolde to batayle wende,
      And hou[19] he hit ouer-com an ende.
1225 ¶ Nas þis a good redes-mon
      Þat[20] vs so deore for-buggen con,

[1] A. ah, H. but. [2] A. hundred. [3] H. omits 'worþ', clearly misunderstanding these two lines, which mean—'For his passion would be nothing worth, were it not for (see Gloss., s.v. Neore) his resurrection.' This couplet is not in the French. [4] A. were. [5] A. resurrexion. [6] A. þow. [7] A. mast. [8] A. bileene. [9] A. forsoþe bileuede. [10] A. ah, H. but. [11] A. mihte. [12] A. were. [13] A. moder. [14] A. maiden. [15] A. now. [16] A. þow. [17] A. for-bouht. [18] A. how, quater. [19] A. gode. [20] V. þan.

CASTEL OFF LOUE.   59

And hap i-rad vs þe way,
Þer vchone of vs þat wole, he may
To þe blisful¹ ioye come
1230 Þ¹ so loge porw Adam² was bi-nome?

Vnderstondeþ³ nou forþere nopeles
Hou he is God and euere⁴ wes,
And ȝe mouwe⁵ openliche i-seon
Þat hit ne may not elles ben.
1235 O God al þe world wrouȝte⁶,
And pulke God vs alle for-bouȝte⁷;
Oþer⁸ God nis non þen he,
Þe God of whom I seide er þe,
Persones þreo in prille-hod.
1240 And o God cleped in on-hod.

Men⁹ may also, clerkes þ¹ cōno¹⁰ reden,
I-seon his Godhede þorw his deden;
For al þe deden¹¹ þat he dude here
W'Godhede and monhede [weore]¹² i-meynt
i-fere.
1245 And nym non ȝeme and þ⁴ miht seon
Hou þat ilke mihte¹³ ben¹⁴.

¹ A. (per sphalma) blisful.   ² 'þorw Adam'; so A., V., and H. But the French reads—
        Ke par cuain fent grant pose
        A tus estupee. e close.
That is, 'which was previously (aupar avant) quite shut (lit. paused), stopped against all, and closed.'   ³ A. onderstodeþ.   ⁴ A. ener.   ⁵ A. mowon.   ⁶ A. wrouhte.   ⁷ A. for-bouhte.   ⁸ A. oþur.   ⁹ A. and H. me, Fr. thos:
        E ses fez pout hom sauoir
        E la puissance deu veeir.
¹⁰ A. cūne.   ¹¹ A. deeden, the last letter very indistinct.   ¹² H. finishes this line with 'he dede in fere'. A. and V. leave the sentence without any verb, for i-meynt can be nothing but a participle. The insertion of weore (or were) seems to be fully justified by the French:
        Kar tut ses fez furent melles
        De hōmasce e de deitez.
¹³ A. mihte.   ¹⁴ A. beon.

Hose hedde a swerd here
þat wel i-steled¹ and kene² were,
And he hit in-to þe fuir dude
1250 þat hit were³ breñynge in þe stude;
Ho is þat penne mihte,
Whon hit barnde so brihte,
þe fuyr⁴ to-delen þe stel fro,
Oþer⁵ þe stel from þe fuir mo?
1255 And hose w⁶ þe swerd smite,
Two kuynden he miȝte⁷ sen⁷ and wite—
þe stel þorw kuynde keruep a-pliht⁸,
And þe fuir brennep⁹ and þ¹ is riht;
And al of o swerd hit come.
1260 Also is of Jhesu Godes sone,
Two kuynden be haþ, we witen bi þon,
Þat he is soþ God and soþ mon.

For alle neces [he schewede] þis priuete¹⁰,
At þe Caane¹¹ of Galylee¹²,

¹ A. i-steeled. ² A. keene. ³ A. weo (sic). ⁴ A. fuir. ⁵ A. oþur.
⁶ A. mihte. ⁷ A. seon. ⁸ A. a-pliȝt. ⁹ V. brande. ¹⁰ A. gives this
line thus:
          For alle neces of þis priuets,
and V. thus:
          For alle neces of þis princes (or princes);
the writer of these MSS.—for we must bear in mind that they are written
by the same hand—having evidently not understood what he was copying.
H. helps us here, reading—
          He shewed gret myracolls and priveté
          At the chaus of Galilé.
The 'for' at the beginning of the line is not in the French, where the
complet—
          As noces selat architeclin
          Kant lasue changat en uin—
seems rather to connect itself with what precedes.
¹¹ A. þe Cane: for the use of the article with this name compare
Maundeville's expression: 'the Cane of Galilee is 4 Myle fro Nazarethe'.
And so in Wiclif's rendering of John 2. 1,—'and the thridde dai wed-
dyngis weren made in the cane of galile' (Engl. Hexapla.) On the other
hand in Rob. de Brunne we have—
          And in Kana Galyle
          He turnede water yn wyne to be. (p. 344.)
¹² A. Galile.

1265 A gistnynge he made Architriclyn¹,
     þer he tornde² water³ to wyn.
     Sixe vessels þer weoren i-don:
     Of water³ he bad hem fulle son;
     [As mon]⁴ he bad don water³ þer-in
1270 And as God he torned hit to wyn.
     And þis ilke dede was al on
     Of sopfast God and sopfast mon.
     And elles-wher⁵ þer he eode,
     Muche folk hī suwede of feole⁶ peode,
1275 Þat fyf⁷ pousend men he hap i-set,
     And w⁸ fyue⁹ loues and twey¹⁰ flasches hem
                                          fed;
     And of þe relef þ¹ hē leuede bi-fore,
     Twelf cupe-ful weoren¹¹ vp i-bore.
     As mon he hem þe bred to-brek¹²,
1280 And as God he hap hem i-fulled ek.

     Of Lazar also þ° miht i-seon eþe
     Hou he him arerede from þe deþe,

---

¹ For this change of a common noun (ἀρχιτρίκλινος) into a proper name, compare Maundevile's words: 'In that Castel, seynt Anne oure Ladyes Modre was born. And there benethe was Centurioes Hous' (p. 117). So we occasionally even now hear and read of the parable of Dives—the syre Dynes of Rob. de Brunne—and Lazarna. So we always speak of Mary Magdalen, though 'Marie Cleophes' (Mand.) is such no longer. But as to the case before us, Wiclif wrote: 'here je to the architriclyn' (Jno. 2. 8). ² V. torned. ³ A. watur &c. ⁴ A. and V. anon. The French is—
     Com hōms emplir les rons
     Com den leawe en vin chāge.
(Rous = rogavit? Kelham has, 'Rosisons, Rogations'.) Compare also with the present passage lines 1279 and 1287 below. In H. we have—
     As by his monhede he bade do watur theryne,
     And by his Godhede he turned the water to wyne,—
conveying the same general sense, though the conjunctions here are all at sixes and sevens. ⁵ H. has 'owher', which clearly = A.S. æghwær, æghwar, ahwær = ever-where = wherever. ⁶ A. fele. ⁷ A. fif. ⁸ A. omits w⁸. ⁹ A. fine. ¹⁰ A. twei. ¹¹ A. waren. ¹² A. to-breek.

Þat foure dawes be leiȝ¹ a-long,
In þe buriles² þat he stonk.
1285 Wiþ loud voys³ he clepede þus:
"Lazar a-ryz and cum out to vs."
Riht as mon he clepede him to,
And as God he a-rerede him also⁴.

In alle his deden me may⁵ wel i-sen⁶
1290 Þat he is God⁷ and euer schal ben⁸.
Þulke God alle þing dihte,
Þat in þe swete Mayden⁹ a-lihte.
Al vre be-leene¹⁰ in him is,
Vre trenþe¹¹ and vre hope i-wis:
1295 Persones preo in prillihod,
And o God panȝ¹² in on-hod.

Nou ȝe habbeþ i-herd witterly
Hou he is God Almihti¹³;
Ac¹⁴ his strengþe ne¹⁵ may no telle,
1300 Herte þenke, ne mouþ spelle.
For þe heiȝe nome Jhesu
Haþ in him so muche vertu
Þat al þat is in heuene hiȝe¹⁶
Abouen and bineoþen¹⁷ feor and neiȝe,
1305 Bouweþ¹⁸ to þilke¹⁹ nome vchon.
For-þi þer ne may bit telle non,
His miht and his strengþe hou hit geþ;
But as a mon þe ryude fleþ²⁰,
Suwhat touchen I chulle fonde
1310 Of þat Ich may vnderstonde²¹.

Þo Adam hedde i-loren þorw synne,
Heuene and eorþe and paradyses²² winne,

¹ A. leih. ² A. buriels. ³ A. vois. ⁴ V. omits *also*. ⁵ A. mal.
⁶ A. i-seen. ⁷ A. þat he was God and is: the Fr. is, kil est deu.
⁸ A. beon. ⁹ A. melden. ¹⁰ A. bi-leeue. ¹¹ A. trouþe. ¹² A.
pauh. ¹³ A. almihty. ¹⁴ H. and. ¹⁵ A. em. ¹⁶ A. heiȝe. ¹⁷ A.
binepen. ¹⁸ A. boweþ. ¹⁹ A. þulke. ²⁰ On this passage see Pr.,
p. 55. ²¹ A. vnderstonde. ²² A. paradys: the form in V. is found

þe fend hedde such miht þo
þat al þe world moste after hi go;
1315 For [whom]¹ þe world was furst wrou3t²,
He haþ him vnder-i-brou3t³.
Such strengþe he him þo ches
þat prince of al þe world be wes.
Þer nas non for his goodschupe,
1320 For penaunce ne for holyschupe⁴,
Þau5⁵ be pynede hi-self in flesch and fellr,
Þat þe fend ne ladde him to helle.

[Ac]⁶ þe strengþe of Jhesu Godes sone
Him haþ al mated and ouer-come.
1325 Ouercome and i-mat he was⁷ ful sone,
Þo he wende of him to done
As he hedde don of oþer alle
þat he lette in-to helle falle:
Alle he ladde herbifore after⁸ his wille,
1330 And In-to helle [con]⁹ hem spille.

To þe croys¹⁰ he con come,
And wolde habben¹¹ his soule i-nome;
Ac¹² ho fayled, þe traytour¹³;
He was a-bated of his tour¹⁴,
1335 For Godes Godhede bi haþ dou cast
In-to helle and i-bounden fast.

also in the Harrowing of Hell, l. 193 (Bodl., MS. Digby 86, fol. 119),
   And comen to paradises blisse.
So in L 211; and in L 173, paralses blisse.
¹ A. and V. whom; H. but for monkynde &c. Fr. is very clear:
   Celui pur ki le munde fu fet
   En son poeir ont attrelt.
² A. wrouht.   ³ A. vnder-i-brouht.   ⁴ A. hollschupe.   ⁵ A. pauh.
⁶ A. and V. and, H. but, Fr. mais.   ⁷ A. was he.   ⁸ A. aftur.   ⁹ A.
and V. com.   ¹⁰ A. crois.   ¹¹ A. habbe.   ¹² H. but yet.   ¹³ A. traitour.
¹⁴ H. anowre, probably because the copyist took tour in the sense of
tower. The line really means, 'he was smitten down in his turn'; compare ll. 1315, 1316. Fr. has—
   Il est de son torn abatuz.

For þorw his Godhede his soule eode
Þidere for hise þat hedden¹ neode,
Þat jore hedden him a-bide
1340 And sore longeden² to gon him mide³.

Helle-jates he al to-breek⁴,
And to-daschte al þe fendes⁵ ek.
A gret bite he bot of helle nom⁶
And drouh alle hise out vchon
1345 Þat leeuede his nome and hī knewe,
And serueden hī wiþ herte trewe.
Such strengþe nas neuer i-berd ar þis,
Ne neuer schal but of him I-wis.
For þe meste strengþe he al bi-reuede
1350 Þat þe feud⁷ in þe world heuede.
He was en-armed ful stronge⁸,

¹ A. hedde. ² A. longede. ³ A. myde. With these lines compare
the words of Adam to Christ in the Harrowing of Hell above referred to:
Welcome lonerd wel þou be
Ful longe hamþ ous þout after þe,
and Eve says,
So longe hanen we ben herinne
Þa fewe nou beþ onre sunne.
⁴ So in the Harr. of Hell:
Helle jates ich come nou to
Nou ich wille þat hy ben bounde
. . .
Helle jates her .I. falle
And suþþen go into helle
Satanas here .I. þe binde
Ne salt þou neuere hene winde
(i. e., never shalt thou unwind). ⁵ A. feondes. ⁶ I strongly suspect
that for *nom* we should read *anon*, as in the form of this line which H.
gives—
The maystri of helle he hede *anon*.
Nom spoils the rhyme, and one would scarcely expect *bot of* = *out of*
except, if at all, in northern English.
⁷ A. feond. ⁸ The scriptural allusion here, namely to the parable of
the 'strong man armed' (fortis armatus, Vulg.) in Luke 11. 21, seems
not to have been understood by the English translator, or even by the
writer of the French MS., who has put *si* where the bishop must have

Þat his pat wuste ful longe¹;
Ac² þo þe strengore hi³ ouer-com,
Gret preye he⁴ him bi-nom.

1355 For-þi him seiþ wol Ysaye,
Þat seiþ in his prophecye
Þat he scholde [Myhtfol]⁵ i-cleped ben⁶.
His strengþe may no mon i-seon,
Ne no tonge ne mihte reden
1360 Ne poujt þenken his mihtful deden.
¶ For his miht me oujte him drede,
And for his swetnes hi⁷ loue ful nede.

Þis is vre child and vre help,
Vre strengþe and vre jelp,
1365 Vre be-leue⁸ and vre socour,
Vre treuþe and vre honour;
Þat so boxum bi-com for vs,
He jaf him-self to sauen vs.
And al o God dude þis,
1370 Fader and Sone and Holigost i-wis.

Sadel je habbeþ i-herd nou riht
Of his stregþe and of his miht;

---

written *li*, both to give point to the allusion and to mark the antecedent
to the relative which begins the next line.
  Li mauſe fu [li] fort arme
  Ki sa porte a si fort garde.
  Mes quant il plus fort sornenelt
  Ses espoilles lui ad toleit.
¹ H. cuts this down into the charming line,
   And wyst full long.
See Pr., pp. 60, 61. ² A. ak, H. bote. ³ A. om. he. ⁴ A. myldeful,
V. myldefol, H. myjhtfull, Fr.—
   Pur ço dit bien ysaie
   En sa douce prophecie.
   Ke *il fort* nome serroit &c.
⁵ A. beon. ⁶ A. be-leeue.

Ac¹ herkneþ¹ ȝit forþere of Ysaye,
Þat cleped² him in his prophecie
1375 Fader of þe world þat acholde come³.
For while he walkede her alle frome,
He fulfulde⁴ in alle þinge
Alle holye prophetes [byddynge]⁵.

Hou he is Fader ȝe schullen⁶ i-heren,
1380 And hou we alle of him i-streoned⁷ were.
Þorw Adam we sugeden furst vchon,
And eeten þe appel wiþ hī anon;
And alle we of him i-streoned⁸ weoren:
Þe cors⁹ þat he beer alle we beeren.
1385 Þorw kuynde we bedden þe curs alle
Þorw riht no miȝt¹⁰ hit elles bi-falle.

Adam vr fader þe forme mon
Flesehliche streoned vs euerichon,
Ac¹¹ þulke fleschliche streonynge
1390 Beere¹² vs bale and serwynge,
Neore¹³ þe grace of swete Jhesu

¹ A. ak, H. but.   ² A. berkeneþ.   ³ A. clepeþ.   ⁴ See note on
l. 65.   The French here is—
                Pere au poeple kl nendroit.
                Au siecle ke fent a uenir.
⁵ A. fulfilde.   ⁶ So Π.; A. and V. have bi-gynnynge, which makes
no sense.   The French is simply 'tute seinte prophecies'. For bidding
= announcement, see Gloss.   ⁷ A. scholle.   ⁸ A. I-stroned his.   ⁹ A.
cors.   ¹⁰ A. miht.   ¹¹ A. ah. In H. this passage is thus metamorphosed :
        And for the synne that Adam in Paradys dede,
        All we that of him come shuld be byn in sory stede,
        Nere the grave [sic] of swete Jhesu
        That us þeynboweht thorgh goddi vertu.
The French is—
                Meis icele engendrure
                Feui a nus e pesme e dure.
                Ne fust la grace Ihesu crist
                Ke nus engendra en esperit.
¹² A. beer.   ¹³ Compare l. 1202.

CASTEL OFF LOUE.

Þat vs strenede¹ [þorw]² gostliche vertu.
Þorw Adam we weore to deþe i-demet³,
Þorw Jhesu vp-rered and al i-qwemed.
1395 He is vre Fader aribt,
And so goodliche vs haþ i-diht
Þ' w' his blod he vs (waschede)⁴ of sinne⁵,
And brou₃t vs out of wo to winne.
Neuer fader for no childe
1400 Of syn loue nas so freo ne mylde.

(Wan)⁶ from þe roode⁷ for vre neode
Riht in-to helle he eode,
Fourti tymen⁸ þer he wes,
[O]⁹ þat he vp-risen ches.
1405 Þat was on þe þridde day,
Erliche vppon a Sones-day,
Þo þe ni₃t¹⁰ fro þe day to-brek¹¹
So scide seint Austin þo he spek¹².
W' him he drou₃ out alle hise
1410 Þat di₃eden¹³ in his seruise
From þe¹⁴ tyme þat be Adam wrou₃te,
Þat he vp-ros¹⁵ and vs for-bou₃te.

To his disciples he bi schewede¹⁶ i-lome¹⁷,
And eet and dronk, eode and come
1415 Fourti dawes he was heere¹⁸ fulliche,
And prechede¹⁹ hem Godes kinericbe.

---

¹ A. streone.   ² A. and V. om.₁ see the readings of H. and Fr. just quoted.   ³ A. i-demed.   ⁴ A. and V. waked, H. wassheth, Fr. laus. See Pr., p. 64.   ⁵ A. synne.   ⁶ Fr. kant: A. and V. have þat. I have no doubt that the earlier manuscript from which A. and V. were copied had the Anglo-Saxon p (w) throughout, and thus the þam = was being mistaken for þas was changed into a conjunction more fitly corresponding to the so in the preceding line, with which this line was connected by mistake. On the p and p compare ll. 287, and 1151, note.   ⁷ A. rode.   ⁸ A. and H. tymes.   ⁹ A. and V. þo, H. er, Fr. deshau liers ior. Line 152 shews pretty clearly what the true reading is.   ¹⁰ A. niht.   ¹¹ A. to-breek.   ¹² A. speek.   ¹³ A. þo þat dyeden.   ¹⁴ A. þat.   ¹⁵ A. s-ros, H. up-ros.   ¹⁶ A. schewed.   ¹⁷ H. sone.   ¹⁸ A. here.   ¹⁹ A. preched.

Vppon holy þoresday¹ þer on his nome
Heo weren³ i-gedered alle i-some
Vppou astude, þer he among hem com,
1420 And of mis-bileue he hem vnderuom.
In whonhope⁴ and doute heo weoren vchon,
ȝit heo sejen hī alyue a lyues-mon.

Þo þt ne mihten heo for no wit⁴
Riht to sope i-leeuen hit.
1425 Ac⁵ heore doute was vre bi-houe⁶,
And fastnede ful wel vre bi-leeue⁷;
For muche vs dude sikernesse⁸
Of Thomas misbileuenesse,
þat nolde for no mon þat was
1430 Bi-leeuen þat he ded and arisen⁹ was,
Ar he bedde bondlet þe woude so wyde,
þat Longeus¹⁰ made in his syde,

¹ A. þorsday.   ² A. weoren.   ³ A. wonhope.   ⁴ i. e. for no wiht
= for nought. See Glossary, s. v. Nouht.   ⁵ H. but jet.   ⁶ A. bibeous.
⁷ A. bileue.   ⁸ A. sihornesse.   ⁹ A. arysen.   ¹⁰ Sic in A. and V.
and the Towneley Mysteries: M. writes Longes, Fr. longis (and so Rob.
the Dev.), the Coventry Mysteries, Longeys, the later Greek and Latin
fathers, Longinus. The origin of the name is apparently implied in the
words 'sed unus militum lancea (λόγχη) latus ejus aperuit', John 19. 34,
Vulg. It is curious to note the various instances in which tradition has
given names to persons who are mentioned but not named in the Scrip-
tures themselves. Thus the mother of the virgin Mary was Anna (see
note on l. 1265), and her father Joachim son of Barpanther, according
to Epiphanius, Greg. Nyss., &c. The magi who visited the infant Jesus,
always reckoned as three in number, are named by Mandeville as 'the
3 Kynges, Jaspar, Melchior, and Balthazar; but Men of Grece clepen hem
thus, Galgalathe, Malgalathe, and Saraphie; and Jewes clepen in this
manere in Ebrew, Appelius, Amerrius, and Damasus.' The readers who
choose to consult Calmet, s. v. Magi, will find this statement as to the
different names given to the three kings by the Jews and the Greeks,
just reversed, as might be expected; and other names also mentioned.
Of the second and third names the Cov. Mysteries give the forms Mel-
chijar and Baltajare, in the latter of which the j probably = z as is occasionally the case. Mandeville again speaking of 'the Cytee of Sarphen'
says, 'and there reysed he Jonas the Wydwes Sone from Dethe to Lyf,'

And¹ scon þe woūdes grene and weet,
Wjuche þat weoren on honden and feet¹.

1435 Þo schewed Jhc² hī his wondes³ wyde
In hondes and feet and pulke on his syde⁴:
"Þou art Ichot"⁵, quaþ Thomas þo,
"Mi God, and my Lord also."
"Ʒe, Thomas," quaþ Jhesu Crist,
1440 "Þou hit leuest, for þou hit sixt;
Alle heo moten i-blessed ben,
Þat hit leeuen, pauȝ⁶ heo hit not seon!"
Openliche he made þulke day
Faste and alker vre [fay]⁷.

1445 Wiþ his disciples he eet þo,
As he was er i-wont to do,
And sette tweyne and tweyne to gon
Ʒond al þe world to precben vchon,
To alle schaft and to alle wihte—
1450 Þat is to mon þorw rihte—
Þat heo bi-loenē⁸ i Godes sone, þ⁹ is in him,
And þat vche mon folwede him⁹

the widow's son not being named by the evangelist himself (Lu. 7. 12).
In like manner the penitent thief—'the gode Theef' (Mand.)—was called
Dysmas, whom Piers Plowman's 'Roberd the Robbere' claims for his
brother (Vis. l. 3419), Dysmas's companion in guilt and punishment being
Jestas according to the Cov. Myst. And the soldiers who had charge of
the grave of Christ receive names in the Cov. Myst. such as appear to
be derived from tradition.

Pylat. Come forth, ȝe ser Amorawnt,
    And ser Arphaxat; com ner also
    Ser Cosdram, and ser Affraunt,
    And here the charge that ȝe must do.

¹ These two lines are omitted in A. ² A. Jhū. ³ A. wondes. ⁴ A.
side. ⁵ A. I wot. ⁶ A. pauh. ⁷ A. and V. lay, H. fay, Fr.—
    A cen lor nout apertisement
    La *foi fermer* de inte gent.
⁸ A. by-leenen. ⁹ That is, had himself *baptized*, see Gloss., and
Pr., pp. 55, 56.

In þe Fader, and in þe Sone also,
And iu þe Holy Gost¹ þat glit of heui bo.
1455 For hose neore i-bore eft, at þe² frome
In-to heuene ne³ miȝte⁴ he neuer come;
Ac⁵ þulke þat beþ⁶ i-folwed in riht bileeue⁷,
Schulen beo brouȝt in Godes bi-heue⁸.

Wel openliche he schewep vs þer-fore
1460 þat vche mon mot eft ben i-bore,
And ȝif we schulen eft i-boren ben⁹,
We mote comen of sunne-streon¹⁰,
þat is þe water of vertu,
þer vs gostliche strenop swete Jhesu;
1465 And whon he vs hap so strened¹¹ i-wis,
Forsoþe vre Fader þenne¹² he is,
And þenne we alle his children beþ.
Sikerliche vnwrustlyche he deep¹³
þat such Fader ne louep w' al his pouȝt.
1470 He ne eet of þe appel riht nouȝt:

¹ A. holigost. ² A. atte for at þe. ³ A. om. ne. ⁴ A. mihte
⁵ A. ak. ⁶ A. beoþ. ⁷ A. bileue. ⁸ Fr. has here—
E lors denisa leur aler
Kil alassent al mud prescher.
A vniuerse creature
Cest a home par droiture.
Kil en le fiz den creussent
E baptizez tonz fenssent.
El nun del pere e del fiz
E del seintisme esperiz.
Kar ki rene ne serrad
Is en ciel nentrerad.
Mes les creanz les baptizez
Serrunt mis en sanctetez.
(I need hardly explain that creanz = belevern, and rene, i. e. rené = born
again, renatus, John 3. 5,—the 'eft i-boren' of our text)   ⁹ A. beon.
¹⁰ FL—
Mes pas ke rene serrom
Engendrure anerum.
¹¹ A. streoned.   ¹² V. om., H. then.   ¹³ A. deþ.

Baldeliche we mouwe[1] þorw hi craue
Vre rihtes in heuene to baue;
For he haþ alle þe lawen[2] i-wyst[3]—
Of o poynt ne haþ he mist—
1475 Þat neuer neore i-wust ne i-bolde,
Er he him-self comen wolde.

Þe forme mon þat of eorþe com,
Brouȝt[4] vs werre and pees bi-nom.
Þat oþer mon from heuene com w' meyn:
1480 And haþ i-ȝolden vre pees[5] aȝeyn.
¶ Fleschliche was þe forme mon,
Þat muche wo vs brouȝte vppon;
Þat was out of paradys i-pult,
And al his ofspring, for his gult.

1485 Ac[6] vre gostlych[7] Fader, swete Jhesu,
Vs bryngeþ[8] aȝeyn þorw his vertu.
He þat from heuene com,
From louh an heiȝ he vs np-nom.
Þat from eorþe com, to eorþe he geþ:
1490 Þat from heuene com, to heuene he step.

¶ On holy[9] þoresday (þer al þe folk i-seiȝ[10]
Wynche[11] þat stoden a-bouten hi neih)
Þe wey he made vs to lede
Þorw þe skewes, þer ho eode
1495 Wiþ sopnesse and wey[12] of liþ[13].

[1] A. mowe. [2] A. and Π lawes. [3] A. i-wist. [4] A. brouht. [5] A. vr pes. [6] A. ak, II. bot. [7] A. gostlich, II. gostill. [8] A. bringeþ. [9] A. holi. [10] A. i-seih. [11] A. whuche. [12] A. wol. [13] Either this passage is corrupt, or the translator has again quite missed the bishop's meaning, whose words are—

        La uoie a ses seins a fet
        Par les nuwes ou il vet.
        Vie. verite. et voie
        Od sei meine bele proie.

'He has made the way for his saints through the clouds where he goes—the life, the truth, and the way. With him he brings a glorious booty.' Here the third line contains an unmistakable allusion to the words, 'Ego sum via et veritas et vita', Jno. 14. 6.

Þe felle cumpanye [he]¹ him laddu wiþ,
Þat he out of helle nom,
Þat to muche blisse com.
To þulke blisse he made hem weende,
1500 Þat euer lasteþ wiþ-outen ende,
Þer he woneþ as he dude er
Wiþ his Fader, o God þer,
Þersones þreo in þrilli-hod²,
And o God þanj³ in on-hod,
1505 Þat alle þing wrouȝte, as þ" mon wost,
Fader and Sone, and Holygost.
Þauj vche nome of þise þre
[He]³ sinderliche⁴ [seyd]⁵ as he ouȝto to be,
O God hit is wiþ-outen care,
1510 Of alle schaftes schoppare;
To whom joye and honour bi-come
Wiþ-outen ende⁶, þe holy Gonse.

Now bisecche we God for his merci
Such lyf her⁷ leden⁷ and so trusti,
1515 Þat we his heste holden so long,
Þulke pes vs wonye among
Þat he sende fro heuene to monkinne⁸.
And þ' he wone w' vs w'-inne;
And aftur⁹ þis lyf to joye wende!¹⁰
1520 Þis writ in God nimeþ¹¹ non ende⁶.
Þer is ende and byginnynge¹²,
So holy writ seyþ¹³, of alle þinge;
God leeue¹⁴ vs here so ende,
Þ' we ben worþi to heuene wende¹⁹. Ame²⁰.

¹ A. and V. om.; II. 'he hadde him wythe'.   ² A. þilly hod (sic).
³ A. þauh.   ⁴ A. synderliche.   ⁵ A. and V. omit the verb; II. has
'hyn syndry seyd', and Fr.—
E all lad distinctian
De trois persones par nnn. &c.
⁶ A. eende his.   ⁷ A. leden her.   ⁸ A. monkynne.   ⁹ A. after.   ¹⁰ A.
weende his. For the to omitted see note on l. 026.   ¹¹ A. nymeþ.   ¹² A.
biginnynge.   ¹³ A. seiþ.   ¹⁴ A. leue.   ²⁰ A. Aþ.

GLOSSARY.

(For words not contained here see Coleridge's Glossarial Index.)

Abate, *v. a.*, smite down, 1334. Fr. abatre.
Abugge (for pronunciation see *Sugge*), *v. a.*, pay the penalty for, 304. A.S. abicgan.
Afterlong, *adv.*, along, 724. Fr. bas—
    De lang is tar e *de Le*,
    i. e. de longo ... de lato.
Agulte, *v. n.*, offend, 335. A.S. agyltan; Fr., in this passage, trespasser. We find *gulte* in the same sense in Moral Ode, 108.
Al, *adv.*, altogether, 524, 1138.
Al, *adj.*, plur. alle, = all, 9, 10, and *passim*. The distinction between the sing. and plur. forms is disregarded in one or other of the MSS. in 18, 333, 433, 545, 561, 850, 1139, 1214.—Oner alle þing=all our things, 12.
Alle and some, = each and all, 469. We have this phrase also in Liber Cure Cocorum, p. 10,
    And hew þy noumbuls *alle and sum*;
and in Handlyng Synne, 160, and 2183, with a noun singular:
    Þe tale ys wrytyn *al and sum*
    In a boke of Vitas Patrum.
In the Play of the Sacrament, l. 402, it undergoes tmesis—
    whyle þa ey were *alle* togethor *and sum*.
Alast, *adv.*, at last, 457, 991. The A.S. expression was *on laste* (compare Aplikt and *I-some*), but the prep. *at* is used in this phrase as early as in Lay. Brut, in which we find *at þan laste* and *a þan laste*, vol. iii, p. 66. If the *a* in *alast* stands for *at*, we may also compare *aiaf* (A.S. *agaf*) as perhaps = *atgaf* = uttered, in the Owl and Nightingale, 139, and A.S. *aspringan*, *odrifan*, *aurípan*, &c. as probably = *atspringan*, &c.
Algate, *adv.*, yet, in any case, at all events, 1085; Fr. totefols.
Amidden, *prep.*, amid, 333. A.S. on middan = in medio.
An, *prep.*, on, 1177, 1488. So often in Lay. Br., and see *End*.
And, *prep.*, = an = on, 1177 (A.), and in like manner
[And-last, *adv.*, at last, 127, A.S. *on laste*. I had put *atte laste* in the

text, and am indebted to Mr. Furnivall for the suggestion of *and-last*. That the reading of the MSS. is corrupt, with *laft* = left, is proved—besides other reasons—by the fact that in this poem all such contracted preterites in -*te* keep the final -*e*, as *ouȝte*, *brouȝte*, *wrouȝte*, *miȝte*, *dikte*, *moste*, &c.]

Anon, *adv.*, 234, 319. The MSS. divide *a non*, though *an on* doubtless is the true division. The A.S. form is *on an* = in one (sc. time, or moment). Even in A.S. the prep. *on* = *in* or *on*, was sometimes written *an*. In Rob. Brunne's Account of Arthur we get the form *on one*:

> Þe messe bigan son *on one*.

In 1083 *al anon* = all in one = all at once.—As to a *non* for *an on*, one case of this kind which seems to have escaped observation is found in Owl and Nightingale, 144,

> Thos hule laste thider-ward,
> And hold hire eje notherwa(r)d,

'kept her eyes turned in another direction'.

Anonden, ?, 1151.
Anont, *prep.*, anent, against, 1076.
Apertement, *adv.*, manifestly, 761.
Apliht, *adv.*, 304, 847, 1058, 1257, certainly, in truth; or more exactly, (in) *plighted* (troth). The prefix *a*, which stands in some cases for *ge*, as in *ago* = *igo* = Germ. *gegangen*, *adight* (Ch.) = *ydight* = A.S. *gediht*, *along* = *ilong* (q. v.) = A.S. *gelang*, *alike* = *yliche* = A.S. *gelic*, (compare *enough* = *ynou* = *genog*),—in others is a corruption of *on* = on or in, as in *alive* (Ch., on live), *abroad* (Ch., on brede), *a-hunting* (Ch., on hunting, and so on *hawking*), *abed* (Ch., on bedde), *aboard*, *afire*, *aloud* (in the Mort Arthure, ed. Hall., one luwde), *anight*, a' *Godes name*; and so Ch. has both *aswoun* and *on swowne*. I suspect that *aplight* belongs to the former of these classes. Mr. Halliwell thinks that it "is the same as 'I plight', I promise you". And we do find 'Mi tranthe I the pliȝte' in the Avowynge of King Arthur, 27. 16, but is there any other instance of the prefix *a* = the pron. *I?*—The explanation 'immediately, at once' given in the Glossarial Index does not suit our passages.

As, *rel.pr.*, which,? 1151. See Furnivall's Early Engl. Poems, p. 77, l. 225.
At, *prep.* governing *gen.*, 92. So to occasionally governs the gen. in A.S. and *of* in Early (and in Modern) English.
At one, 402. Taking this reading as in the MSS., the *ene* must = the earlier *æne* from the numeral *an*, one. Then *at ene* will = at once, though in the old form of this phrase (*at ones*) the preposition governs the genitive; see *At*. In La̧. Br. *æne* is either dat. or acc., and *at* regularly takes a dative. The *at* redundant before *at ene* is paralleled in *as tyte* (Handl. Synne, l. 264), *assrype* (ib. 1452), and many of Chaucer's adverbial phrases, especially of time, such as *as now*, *as at this time*, *as for that day*, *as in his tyme*, &c.

But I suspect the genuineness of the reading, though emendation is not easy. My friend the Rev. J. Earle suggests *as at-gene* in the sense of 'and that for certain'. He says: "It sounds to me as if *at-gene* is a good representative of the old inflected *gegnum* = obviam: *gegnunga*, adv., aperte, certe, omnino, plane, prorsus, (Grein, s. v.); and compare the provincialism 'the gainest way' = the nighest way." The *jene* of O. and N. 843 which is unexplained in the Gloss. Ind. is apparently a verb, and = meet.—Were the existence of a verb to *atgive* (see *Alast* and *Atsprong*) established, I should be inclined, by aid of II., to read—

Þis þral of whō my enelren menē
Hap dom deserued as at-jenē,

i. e. as already pronounced.

At one (in the MSS. *a ton*) = agreed, 492, 493. The fuller phrase *atte one assente* occurs in the Avowynge of King Arther, 52. 9, and in the Seven Sages, 1. 2072 (*at on acens*); while we find also *at on red* in nearly the same sense in l. 2064 of the latter poem. (Qy. When did the verb *atone* first appear in its modern sense, or, as in Shakspere, in the sense of *to reconcile*?)

At-sprong, *part.*, sprung, descended, 152, A.S. asprungen. There is an A.S. noun *atspringnes*, springing out, given by Bosworth.

Atset, *v.a.*, put away, set aside, neglect, 235.

Atter, *sb.*, gall, 1150. Fr. has *fel amer*, II. *galle*; though A.S. *atter* or *ator* = poison.

Awayte, *v.a.*, lie in wait for, 767. The French is—

Ki nos *agueitent* tut dis.

Cotgr. has *aguetter*, Palsgr. *aguayter*, for to lie in wait.

Baldeliche, *adv.*, boldly, 1081, 1471.

Bat, *v.a.*, biddeth = prayeth, Fr. huche, 884. A.S. bit, from biddan. See *Forbat* and *Hat*.

Bayle, *sb.*, 687, 805. 'Bailey, a name given to the courts of a castle, formed by the spaces between the circuits of walls or defences which surrounded the keep. Oxf. Gloss. Arch.' Halliwell's Arch. Dictionary. 'Baille, pieu, palissade'. Ménage.

Be, beo (= by, as in H.), *prep.*, concerning, as to, 495. So *be* in A.S., as, cwepan to þā menigu *bi* Johanne, Rushw. Goep., Mt. 11. 7.

Beclepe, *v.a.*, complain of, appeal against, 498.

Begot, *v.a.*, gain, profit, part. bi-jeten, 1126.

Beheste, *sb.*, promise, 336. Fr. has—

La *primesse* lui fauserent.

Bel), beth, *v.a.*, pret. of bow, 358. A.S. bugan, pret. beah, beag.

Bend, *v.a.*, = circumdare, as in the modern nautical expression 'the sails are bent', 743.

Berbican, *sb.*, barbican, 697, (823). The *barbican* was an outwork—'one faussebraye, ou muraille de dehors, *antemurale*. On appeloit aussi

76 GLOSSARY.

barbacanes les défenses qu'on faisoit au bout d'un pont,' (Ménage).
See also Viollet-le-duc's Military Architecture in the Middle Ages,
especially figures 17 and 18. But the name *barbican* was also, according to Ménage (and Spelman), applied to the 'meurtrières' or
machicoulis, (for which see Viollet-le-duc, figures 19 and 68) 'c'est-à-
dire ces ouvertures qui sont aux murailles des villes et des places
fortes, d'où l'on tire à coups de mousquet sur les ennemis.' But of
barbacan in this sense I can find no example in any old writer, or
in any of the dictionaries. It is worth observing also that the strange
blunder of confounding *barbacan* with *crenean* is found only in one
or two modern writers (Vigénère quoted by Ménage, and Raynouard).
In our author, l. 823, the case is simply one where 'bonus dormitat
Homerus', as the words 'þe sene' prove to a demonstration: the
ἀναφορά of the definite article being to 'seven barbicans' already
mentioned (l. 697), whereas no 'seven battlements' are mentioned.

Bealht, *sb.*, award (?), 311. Fr.,
Par *agard* de jugement.
Bespeak, *v. a.*, threaten (?), 721.
Bi-caste, *v. a.*, surround, part. bi-caste, 694.
Bicome, *v. a.*, belong, 1511. Fr. apent (Lat. appendet) = appartient.
Bid, *v. a.*, desire, 1006.
[Byddynge, *sb.*, announcement, 1378. Compare the use of the verb
beodan in Beowulf, l. 786, and Cædm., p. 188, 11.]
Bifal, *v. s.*, belong, 81, 293, 928.
Bifoule, *v. a.*, defile, 1147.
Bihere, *sb.*, behoof, advantage, 1435. A.S. bihefe.
Bille, *v. a.*, belong, 96, 293. A.S. *belicgan* = extend or lie, by or about.
Bi-loke, *part.*, locked up, 992.
Bi-reve, *v. a.*, take away, 1349. A.S. bereafian.
Bipouht, *part.* from A.S. beþencan = remember, 482. The Fr. is—
E por moi aneir *retreit*,
i. e. 'and to have me brought back' viz. *to mind*. (Compare Fr. l. 556
Com avant none ai *retret*,
'as before I have *reminded* you'.) Bi-pouht = considered, devised, 698.
Blyntzherved, *part.*, blindfolded, 1146. The *whervet* is from A.S. *hweorfan*, to turn, or the noun *hweorfa*, a whirl, a spool.
Boffet, *sb.*, buffet, blow with the open hand, 1148. Fr. hes—
E des *paumes* le *ferirent*.
Bond, *sb.*, bonds, confinement, 1095.
Borwe, *v. a.*, protect, save, 829. Is not *borwe* in this sense derived from
A.S. *beorgan*, though of the same form as the derivative from *borgian*?
So the *folwe* of our poem is not A.S. *folgian* but *fullian*.
[Bot, *v. a.*, pret. of bite, 1343: see note. A.S. bítan, pret. hát. He
bote hys lyppys, Emp. Oct., l. 1070]
Bopé, *num. adj.*, both, 497. A line of five syllables in this metre would

GLOSSARY. 77

scarcely be tolerable; but the A.S. *árgen*, O.Sax. *berle*, Du. and Ger. *bride*, &c., fully warrant us in taking the word as a dissyllable.
Bote, but, *conj*, unless, 250, 374.
Bote, but, *conj.*, used where we should now use the unemphatic *why*, 809. So *allá* often in Greek, as in Rom. G. 6.
Breer, *sb.*, had (?), 183.
Breme, *adj.*, rampant, furious, 501, 538.
Bugge (for pronunciation see *Sugge*), *v.a.*, buy, 1091.

Care, *sb.*, 217, sorrow, grief, distress,—*chagrin*, Palsgr. Such is the true sense of this word in Early English, and not solicitude or anxiety. The phrase 'cark and care' is not simply 'acribus sollicitæ mentis curis confici' (Jun.), in which case it would be a mere tautology. Thorpe's rendering of 'on eararum cwidum' by 'with anxious speeches' (Cædm. p. 269, l. 2) does not at all express the force of the passage: it should rather be 'sorrowful' or 'lamentable'. In l. 1500 care = doubt.
Careful, *adj.*, sorrowful, 463.
Carfulleche, *adv.*, sorrowfully, 903.
Carnel, *sb.*, (in this poem) a battlement, 695, 806, (823). The modern *créneau*—for beyond doubt it is the same word—is defined by Chambaud 'une de ces pièces de Maçonnerie, coupées en forme de dents, et separées l'une de l'autre par intervalles égaux, au haut des anciens murs de ville ou de château.' So 'piana muri' is Carpentier's explanation of *carnellus* and *quarnellus*, and Ducange gives the same both for *quarnellus* and for *ngrrellur*. But Barthius (ap. Ménage) gives a very different definition: 'foramina quadrata in muris et munitionibus'. And so in Grassi's Dizionario Mil. Ital. *créneau* is given as the Fr. equivalent of 'archibusiera: picciola apertura, che si fa ne' muri per tirare coll' archibuso contro il nemico;'—only the *archibusiera* (archière) is not a 'foramen quadratum', but a long and narrow slit, made perpendicularly in a wall or brattish, (see Viollet-le-duc's Mil. Arch. In the Middle Ages, Macdermott's translation, p. 40). We have then two meanings for this word: *battlement* and *loophole*. In the latter sense only is the word, in the form *crenelle*, used by Mons. Viollet-le-duc in the work just quoted; and in that sense we have *cranel*, *cranal*, and *crenel* in passages from the Romance writers quoted by Raynouard, and *kernews* in the Conquest of Ireland, l. 2330. And it is somewhat surprising to find 'battlements' given by Mr. Morton as the rendering of this word in 'ipen open *kernel*', and 'þe *kernewes* of þe castel beoð him huses þurles', Ancren Riwle, p. 62. 'Battlements' are not windows; the sense is, 'the *loopholes* of the castle are the windows of their houses'. Such is also the meaning where we read of 'quatuor homines ad unumquemque *carnellum* custodiendum', (document cited by Carpentier). And in the Mort Arthur, ed. Hall., p. 256,

The cowntas of Crasyne
with hir clere maydyns
Knells downe in the *kyrnellen* &c.

Where mention is made simply of a 'mur *quernele*', (and compare P. Pl. Vis., l. 3682) it is often not easy to say which kind of crdnean is signified; but in Napier's History of the Peninsular War a 'crenellated wall' means always, I believe, a battlemented wall. And so in our poem the *carnels* which

.... stondep vp-ribt,
Wel i-planed &c.

are shown to be battlements not loopholes by the epithet in the French '*gran kerneaus*'—for great size may be an advantage in battlements, not in loopholes—and by their being on the top of the wall, 'par enson', see the lines quoted on p. 32. And in the St. Graal (vol. 2, p. 386, l. 439) the *kernels* are masses of masonry one of which might fall down and kill a man,—

And as sone as vnder the yate was he gon,
On hym there fyl a grot *kernel* of ston,
And ouercovered hym bothe toppe and to.

Cmt, *v.a.*, to trace the design of, to plan, 807. Compare i-prowen, 739.
Catel, *sb.*, chattels, 990.
Ches, pret. of choose, = obtained, 1317. But this abuse of the word is simply due to the exigency of the rhyme.
Cleche, *v.a.*, lay hold of, take, 734. Probably another form of *clutch*.
Con, *v.a.*, knows, understands, 555. Fr. has—

Cil ki cest ensample *entent*.

And compare Chaucer's lines,

In alle the ordres foure is noon that can
So moche of daliaunce and fair langage.

Con, 387, = gon, q. v.
Congraffet, 1056, imitation of the French *cyrografes* = confirmed, registered. See Pr., pp. 54, 55.
Covring (H. kevering), *sb.*, recovery, 672.
Cudde, *v.a.*, pret. of kype = make known, show, 756. A.S. cypan, pret. cydde. In the Moral Ode, st. 97, we have

Mochele inne he us *cudde*;

and in Judicium, p. 16, the part. occurs,

To me was that unkyndnes *kyd*.

Compas, *sb.*, circle, 739. Compare R. Brunne's account of the Round Table:

Non wist who of pan most was,
For pei sat alle in *compas*.

Cupe-ful, *sb.*, basket-ful, 1278. Fr. has 'doze *coffins*', and the Greek of St. Matthew, 14. 20, *Judexa κοφίνους πλήρεις*.

Dar, *v.n.*, = par = needs, used personally, 733, V., but A. has par impersonal.

Darston = A.S. þearft þu = needest thou, 975.
Depeynted, part., coloured, 704. Fr. has depeint.
Disseysed, part., delivered, 1088; but this line is a mistranslation of the French, which is—
No serrai a tort deseisi,
'I shall not be wrongfully dispossessed'.
Do, v.a., = make, 739.
Do, v.a., give, impart, 1427.
Drihte, sb., lord, 27. The A.S. nominative was sometimes monosyllabic, but sometimes drihten or dryhten was used, as in Tat. we find trohtin and truhtin, and in Isid. Hisp. druhtin. It follows that the final e of drihte, as perhaps representing the termination en, may be sounded, if the metre requires it.
Drouh, dronj, v.a., pret. of draw, 1344. A.S. dragan, pret. drog or dröh.
Dunt, sb., dint, blow, 1161.

Eft, adv., again, 751, 1455, 1460. A.S. æft, eft.
Eisil, sb., vinegar, 1150. A.S. aisil, eisile.
Elisen, pr.n., Eliasæus, Elisha. Between the forms Elisen and Elisen (V.) we can easily decide, guided by the analogy of Matthew, Andrew, Bartholomew, Grew (or Gru q. v.) from Matthæus, &c.
Enarmed, part., armed, 1351.
End, sb. 1 on end = at the last, finally, 572, 973, 1011, 1224; = to the end, completely, 1064. In 1177 we have an ende = on end in the former sense; and Bunyan uses the same expression in the latter sense when Honest exclaims, 'Knew him! I was a great Companion of his: I was with him most an end.' (Pilgr. Progr., Hansard Knollys edition, p. 297.)
Eorne, ern, v.n., run, 726, 730. A.S. yrnan.
Eorþe, sb., earth, as a fem. noun, 95.
Er þon, conj., before that, 492. Just so in Tat., c. 17. 5, we have er thanne = priusquam.
Even, adj., just, equitable, 488, 490.
Eþe, adv., easily, 1281.
Evencristen, sb., neighbour, Fr. prome (proximus) = prochain, 976.
Ever-ilte, adv., always, 342. Fr. has tut tens. Everyet, which occurs also in Ancren Riwle, p. 52, seems to have as good a claim to be one word as evermore, which we have in 355.
Eyle, adv., evil, 223.

Feirleh, sb., beauty, 145, 672. See Transactions for 1862-3, pp. 46, 47. To the list of words of this form given in Mr. Fry's paper add merylake, Judkinm, p. 18.
Feirschipe, feirschope, sb., beauty, 690, 747.
Feore, sb., equal, companion, 483, 1091. A.S. fera, Lat. (in accordance with Grimm's law) par.

GLOSSARY.

Folls, v.a., to contend with, 430. But the A.S. feohtan, with which this
fettep, if the true reading, must be connected, is not an active but
a neuter verb; and its primary meaning, to sing, and hence to contend
in song, seems but ill suited to the passage before us. See note.

Fey, feij, sb., union, 467. A.S. gefeg.

Fynliche, adv., purely, 1132.

Fleschliche, adv., carnally, 1389.

Folful, v.a., complete, 561.

Folwe, v.a., baptize, 1452, 1457. A.S. fulllan, fulwian, Et Mark. fulhen,
Orm. follhtnenn.

Fon on, v.a., = attack, 895. The same use of this word occurs in Laj.
Brut. Halliwell gives foe also as = fall in the Lanc. dial.

For, prep., notwithstanding, 1013. The sense is: 'But I stay not to say
how, for all that, a good man may &c.' Compare Handl. Synne,
l. 3162, and

In soche aventure y was to day
That a rybawde had me borne away
For alle my knyghtys kene. Emp. Octav., l. 1062.

And in Chaucer's Tale of the Doctor of Phisik,

This mayde schal be myn for my man.

See also the Morte Arthur, ed. Hall., p. 242, 2.

Forbat, v.a., forbiddeth, 1005. See Bat.

Forbagge (for pronunciation see Sugge), v.a., redeem, 1090. Part. forbonjt,
1906.

Fore, sb., = A.S. fær, for, for: of pat fore = how it fared with him = of
that suffering, 1156.—Or perhaps = decease, death, as the verbs faran
(cf. l. 218) and ferian are used = to die. (Suggested by Rev. J. Earle.)

Forlete, v.a., lose, 178.

Formest, adv., first; Fr. primes; 1140. So formeste in Friesic, as an
adj., Rechtsqn., p. 40.

Forschippyng, sb., deformity, 640.

Forschipte, part., deformed, misshapen, 634. A.S. forsceapen.

Forte = for to = to, with an infin., 1082, 1126.

Forpfare, v.n., go forth, go one's way, 218.

For-jemed, part., gone astray, Fr.esgarez, 947. From A.S.forgyman=transgress.

Frome, sb., beginning: atte frome (with a negative) = at all, Grk. ἀρχήν,
1455. So frome alone is used in—

Frome loughe none tylle late nyght,
Bot gyffen many a wofull wounde.

Mort Arth. (Rnnb. Cl.), p. 49.

Frovere, v.a., comfort, 889. A.S. frofrian, and see Gloss. Ind. Other
forms from the same root with l for the first r, are Tatian's fluobra
and fluobara = consolatio, fluobiren = consolari, and fluobar geist
= spiritus consolationis. The frowere of our text seems to be the
subj., = shall comfort; compare habbe, 928.

GLOSSARY. 81

Garysoun, sb., healing, restoration to health, 870. Kelham gives *garis* in the sense of the modern *guérir*, and see note on l. 889.
Gadering, sb., combination, union, 643. A.S. gaderung.
Get, v.a., part. *i-gete*, 1070. But see note.
Gyn, sb., engine, ingenuity, skill, 680, 698. Lat. ingenium. Fr. has *engin* in each place.
Gladynge, sb., cheerfulness, 841. Fr. has *liesce* = liesse.
Glide, v.n., proceed (of the Holy Ghost), 1454. Pres. Ind. 3. sing., glit.
Godhede, sb., godhead, deity, 81. The A.S. word was *godcundays*.
Gome, sb., Being, (applied to God), 1512.
Gon, v.n., = began, or begins; often used with an infinitive following as equivalent to the simple verb, as in 709, 885. In the second of these it is plainly a present tense.
Goodliche, adv., excellently, 1396.
Goodschipe, sb., goodness, good thing, 16, 603. In A.S. the form *godnes* was used, and apparently not *godscipe*.
Gostliche, adj., spiritual, 841.
Gostliche, adv., spiritually, 1464.
Gru, sb., Greek, 24. Compare Mandevile, p. 76, 'and there *uyghe* .... is this writen in *Grew*: 'Ο θιὸς &c.'

Hat, v.a., commandeth, 1008. A.S. hæt, from batan.
Hateliche, adj., odious, ill-favoured, 682. A.S. hatigendlic, atelic.
He, of things, 40, 738.
Helle-yates, sb., the gates of hell, 1341.
Helle, v.n., was called, 300; A.S. hel, pret. of hatan, Germ. heissen.
Hevene-blisse, sb., the bliss of heaven, 113.
Hevene-bowe, sb., Fr. arc du ciel, 743.
Hevene-drihl, sb., heaven's Lord, 225, (915).
Hevene-kyng, sb., the King of heaven, 344.
Hi,te, v.a., = promised (of evil), threatened, 176. Compare Pricke of Consc., 107.
Ho, *interr. pron.*, who, 1159, 1251. See *Who*.
Holigost, sb., the Third Person of the Trinity, 7.

I-coren, part. of choose, A.S. gecoren, 203.
I-cussen, v.a., collateral form of *kiss*, 59.
I-diched, adj., protected by a ditch, 674.
I-dut, part., shut, 31. From A.S. *dyttan*, to close or shut up: so *dit*— a word "still used in the North". (Halliwell).
[I-gete, v.a., gain, A.S. begitan, 1070, where see note. Many such by-forms, with the prefixed *i*- derived from the A.S. *ge*-, are found in La3. Br., Ancren Riwle, &c., as *uelen* and *iuelen* = A.S. gefelan, *winden* and *iwinden* = A.S. gefindan, *seli* and *iseli* = A.S. gesælig, *ðolien* and *iðolien* = A.S. geþolian, &c.]

f

GLOSSARY.

I-hear, v. a., collateral form of *hear*, 418. A.S. gehyran.
I-know, v. a., collateral form of *know*, 29. In A.S. *cnawan* has the by-form *gecnawan*, though *cnawan* apparently has none such.
I-let, part., = A.S. *gelagod*, made law? 169.
I-limed, adj., furnished with limbs, 624.
Ilong, adv., along, 229. *Ilong on* is here used in the sense of *along of*, i. e. owing to, in consequence of, as in Shakspere's Cymbeline, 5. 5,
    O she was naught, and *'long of* her it was
    That we meet here so strangely.
So in Scott's Lay of the Last Minstrel:
    Dark Musgrave, it was *long of* thee.
Bosworth quotes two examples of *gelang on* in the same sense.
Inde, sb., indigo, 712.
Inemmste, adj., inmost, 809.
Insiht, sb., understanding, knowledge, 276. The Fr. is—
    De bon noleir. de grant savoir.
I-planed, part., built with a smooth face, 676, 696.
I-rod, part. of rede, to advise, 1227.
I-see, v. a., collateral form of *see*, 16, 556. A.S. *ge-seon*. Pret. i-sei), 319.
I-some, adv., together, 1418. In the Gloss. Ind. this word is derived from the A.S. *gesam*; but this seems not to exist as a separate word. The true derivation is shown in—
    His moder and he dwellyd *in same*. Weber, Ipomydon, 1555.
The prep. *at* was used in this phrase in A.S.—*ealle ætsomne*. Compare *Atast*.
I-steled, adj., made of steel, 1248.
I-vet, 310, = at enmity, participial adj. from A.S. *fah*, *gefah*, = foe, or from the abstract *fahðe*, *fagð*, Isl. *fard*, &c. (see Bosworth) = feud, enmity. The same word occurs in Sir Perceval as *fade*, and in Lai. Brut as *ifuried*, *iuuried*, *iued*, *iveipet*, &c. See Sir F. Madden's Glossary, and Glossarial Remarks, p. 448.
I-wite, v. a., collateral form of *wit* = know, 67. A.S. *gewitan*.

Justise, sb., a judge (apparently), 550. But Fr. reads, e banks justice spent.
Justise, v. a., govern, 298. Compare—
    Whan Arthore had his land *Iustised*. Rob. de Brunne's Chronicle, Inner Temple MS. fol. 62, col. 1 (Pref. to *Handlyng Synne*, p. xxxviii).

Kevering, sb., recovery, 950.
Kinewurpe, adj., royal, 14. From A.S. *cyne* of the same meaning. Lajamon has the compound, like our author.
Kulpe, v. a., show, Fr. montrer, 590, 756. A.S. cyðan. See *Cudde*.
Kuynde, sb., nature, 1179.
Kuynde, adj., natural, 1044.
Knyndeliche, adj., natural, 193.

Knn, sb., kind; see note on l. 855.

Ledene, sb., language, speech, 32. A.S. lyden.
Lende, v. a., dwell, tarry, 604.
Leste, part., lost, 1058. Compare lesten in Halliwell's Arch. Dictionary.
Leve, v.a., grant, 1593.
Leve, v.n., remain, 1277. Compare—
  Quen alle his men was partutte him fro,
  The knyjte lafte stille in alle the woe,
  Bi him seluen allone. Sir Amadace, 33.
Lintel, sb., door (?), 77.
Lyvesmon, sb., living man, 1422.
Lodliche, adv., grievously, 1136. A.S. laðlice.
Lof-song, sb., song of praise, 29. A.S. lof-sang, O.Du. lof-sanch, Germ. lob-gesang, Dan. lovsang.
Lond, sb., = the earth, the world, 551, 654. Fr. has en terre twice.
Lordschipe, sb., 142.
Loyte, adj., little, 632.

Maat, adj., check-maled, defeated, 831, 1205. Fr. mate, which is the modern Fr. maté.
May, aux. v., = can, possum, Germ. können, 1; mowe, 23. Fr. has puet in l. 1, poent in the latter passage.
Maystrie, sb., mastery, victory, 908; force, violence, 1098.
Makeles, adj., matchless, 819.
Mester, sb., business, function, 478. Fr. mestier, métier; Aucren Riwle, meister.
Meyne, sb., main, power, 1479.
Mildful, adj., full of mildness, 367, 643 (V.).
Mis-biled, part., misled, 428.
Misbilevenesse, sb., unbelief, 1426.
Mis-lrad, part., ill advised, 427.
Mislyken, adv., in various ways, 947. A.S. mislæclic, mislænlic.
Mitte = mid þe = with thee, 399.
Monbede, sb., manhood, humanity, 1244.
Monkynne, 670, Monkonne, 1168, sb., mankind. Compare Cædmon's engel-cynna = angel-tribes, p. 16, [14], and the Angelcyn = English race, of the Angl. S. Chron.
Moste = must, used elliptically, 220. Compare the lines from the fable 'Of þe Vox and of þe Wolf', MS. Digby 86,
  Adoun he moste: he was perinne:
  I-haut he wes mid swikele ginne.
Mote, expressive of a wish, 1441. See the Fr., Aient il &c. Compare also—
  Brünt leve óm, wilkomen móte ji wæsent B. de F., p. 18.
So myjte is used in Av. of K. Arther, 18, 9.

Mengen, v.a., mention, 1193. A.S. myngian.

Neces, sb., nuptials, wedding, 1963. Fr. noces.
Nede, neode, sb., need, 19: neode to = need of, ibid.
Nempne, v.a., name, 299.
Neore = ne were = were it not for, 1202 (see note), and 1391. We have
the same idiom in Chaucer's Prologe of The Nonne Prestes Tale,—
  For sicurly, ner gingling of the bellis
  That on your bridil hoog on every syde,
  By heven king that for us alle dyde
  I scholde or this hen falle doun for sleep.
Niman, v.a., used reflexively = to betake, addict, devote (oneself), 772.
Fr. hers is se prist. In 959 the same verb is used passively in the
same sense.
No, adv., 1099.
No, conj., nor, b (A.).
Noubt, noujte, sb., 34. The received derivation of this word as = no
wikt is confirmed by the expression in Tat., ni unas wikt gitanes,
factum est nihil, c. 1, 2; and, nio wikt mer, nihil amplius, c. 15, 17.
And see 1098 and 1423 of our poem, with which compare—
  Ector ne liked that no wight,
  The wordis that he herd there. Mort Arth. (Roxb. Cl.), p.16.
Nouþer, prom., neither, 425.
Nuy, sb., mischief, annoy, 442, 553. Fr. ennui; Rom. nueis, enueia,
enney, &c.

O, conj., until, 152, (1404). A.S. oð. The o þat of our text is equivalent
to the A.S. oð þat, as in Gen. 27.45, quoted by Bosworth, and to
the oðet, aðet, aðat, of the Ancren Riwle. With the present passage
compare—
  Thon shalt buen in bondes ay
  O that come domesday. Harrowing of Hell, (Hall.), l. 136.
and l. 146 of the same poem.
Of, prep., in the case of, 366 (where see note), 485, 646, 1260, 1281, 1326.
On, prep., = in, 74. In Piers Pl. Vis., l. 8176, we have the now usual
form 'in Englisshe', followed by 'on Englishe' nine lines below.
On, conj., until, 472. As o stands often for on (the numeral one), so
here on seems to stand for an entirely different o, viz. o = A.S. oð.
See O.
Onde, sb., 211, 315, 443, 902: see notes on the second and fourth of
these passages. The true meaning of the word is very evident when
we compare, 'þe prid sin so is onde', Early Engl. Poems (ed Furn.),
p. 70, with 'þe pryde aynne ys enuye', Handl. Synne (ed. Furn.),
l. 3918. The Danish form of apparently the same word is avind
= envy, rancour, spite; and in the French of our poem, l. 268, we have

GLOSSARY. 85

Ki par promesse le trahirent
Par mal trespasser le firent.

There is also a Danish *adj. ond* = wicked, malignant.
One, *adv.*, alone, only, 1050. Compare Mort Arth. (Roxb. Cl.), p. 11,
When they come by them one two
Of his helms he takis thore.

So *ein* is used in Tat., as, In themo *einen* brote al libet ther man
= in *solo* pane non vivit homo; Inti imo *einemo* thionos = et illi
soli servies.

Onhod, *sb.*, unity, 10, 1240, 1504, &c. The A.S. form was *annes*, *annys*,
or *anes*, i. e. *oneness*. In Pricke of Consc. we have *anhede* = this *onhod*.

Otewyse, *adj.*, hateful, 1151. This, and the A.S. *atelic*, (the *atelicke* of
our poem, l. 682), seem to contain the same root as *hate* and Lat.
odi. The termination is the same as in the adjectives *rihtwis*, *wrongwis*,
unwlylwys (Pr. of Conscience), &c.

Oper, *adj.*, second, 1479. So in A.S., and in Friesic, as—'Secunda petitio: Thet is thin *other* kest', Rachtsqu., p. 2.

Over-al, *adv.*, everywhere, 732. Old Saxon overal, Germ. überall.

Over-flee, *v.a.*, overflow, 849.

Overgart, *adv.*, presumptuously, 693. The same word occurs twice as a
subst. in Seinte Marherete; see Mr. Cockayne's Glossary, p. 106.

Over-wrije, *v.a.*, cover over, 718. See *Wrey*.

Outriht, *adv.*, entirely, quite, 263.

Outjong, *sb.*, = outgang, outgoing, Lat. exitus, 878.

Parlument, *sb.*, conference, 897.
Pass, *v.a.*, trespass, 1057.
Pite, *sb.*, pity, compassion, Fr. pitié, 353.
Privete, *sb.*, peculiar nature or power, 1263.
Pult, *part.*, thrust, 207.

Qwarel, *sb.*, 826, explained in Gloss. Ind. as = arrow. Is it not rather
a square or four-sided bolt for a cross-bow?
Quit, *adj.*, free, 1142. In Old Saxon *kwyt*, as,
Do worden wi siner ene wila *kwyt*,
'then were we quit of him for_a time'; Reineke de Fos, p. 12.

Rede, *v.a.*, tell, explain, *part.* I-rad, 654. A.S. rædan, part. geræded, ræd.
Rede, *v.a.*, declare, tell, 1359.
Redeful, *adj.*, wise in counselling, 612.
Redesmon, *sb.*, counseller, 1225.
Relef, *sb.*, remainder, 1277. Fr. relef.
Reles, *sb.*, release, relaxation, pleasure, rallah, 509. Kelham gives 'Relais,
release, relaxation', and in a kindred sense Chaucer uses the verb in
I pray you alle my labour to *relesse*.

In the sense of *pleasure* or *relish* we have the subst. In

  Il n'y a nul de tel relers
  come de femme un dous baysor,

Wright's L. P., p. 9. And so in one poem. For the change of sibilant compare *lees* = leash in Chaucer, as 'holdeth in a *lees*', Sec. Nonnes Tale.

Reupful, *adj.*, rueful, sad, 197.

Rue, *v.a.*, used personally, = excite pity in, cause to pity, 540, 541. H. has *rueth* impers. in each line. Tat. has *riuua* = pœnitentia, and H. de F. *ruwe* = Reue, Kummer.

Savete, *sb.*, safety, salvation, 354, 944. Fr. sauvetes.

Saujt, saubt, *adj.*, soft, gentle, 459, 520, and 552. Akin to this are the A.S. sæht, sahte, sahtlian, sahtnys, soft, &c., Germ. sacht, sanft, Du. zacht, and in Kil. saecht and saft, Da. sagte, &c. Saubt = reconciled, 52. Compare Some.

Saubten, *v.a.*, reconcile, 546, 933. A.S. sahtian, sahtlian.

Saubtcasse, sanjtnesse, *sb.*, softening (of enmity), reconciliation, 474. A.S. sahtnys. *Sagtmode* appears in the same sense in Rein. de Fos, p. 45, and *Saghtel* in Pr. of Consc., L 1470.

Sawe, *sb.*, story, 619.

Say, *v.n.*, = speak, 860. H. has 'that God *spak* of'.

Say, *v.n.*, tell, 337. So *secyan* often in A.S.

Schaft, *sb.*, origin, birth, 661. A.S. gesceaft, sceaft.

Schappare, *sb.*, (shaper), Creator, 1510. A.S. sceoppend.

Sell, *v.a.*, deliver, give, 344. Bosworth contends for this as "certainly the first and the oldest signification" of the A.S. *syllan*, Mœs. *saljan*, &c. In the Lindisf. and Rushw. Gospels we have *sealdon* or *saldun* = *dederunt*, in MatL 27. 34. And that such is the meaning in the passage before us is tolerably clear from the French—

  E le prison a moi *rendu*,

while the writer of H. also transforms the line into—

  And the prisoner thou *jeve* to me.

Serwynge, *sb.*, sorrow, 1390.

Set, *v.a.* Lawe *set* or *i-set* = positive law as opposed to moral or natural law, 170, 193.

Shall, used elliptically, 719. Many instances might be quoted of this use both of *shall* and of other auxiliaries; but it is most usually *go* which is understood, as in L 220, in Handl. Synne, l. 2484, and in Early Engl. Poems, 3. 33,

  glad was þe deuil wol to I-wit. for þe sorow þat he *sold* to.

And compare p. 19. 37: also this—

  Forstát dit wol, It is jo onlte,
  Jl *sholen* dárben nnde ok myn frnwe;

Reineke de Fos, p. 83. But it is otherwise in p. 93 of the same poem,

De Koning sprak: wal skal de rym
Unde de folen unnuiten word &c.?
l. e., 'What shall this nonsense mean?'- In the Moral Ode, 67, we have
ac þe þe nout naned ibet. wel muchel he scal beten,
i. e., 'But he who has not amended, severely shall he be beaten.'
Siker, *adv.*, certainly, 685.
Skewes, *sb.*, clouds, 1404. Fr. nuwes.
So, *conj.*, = as, 104, 722, 764. This use of so is not very uncommon
in Early English, and is found also in Anglo-Saxon. Here are other
examples from kindred dialects. '.... so is deer in der wnld cael
so swells soe dat godes ryck'; Old Frisian Laws (Westerl. Landr.).—
'Wo Reinke sprikt ..... unde spriki so hyr folget'; Reineke de Fos
(Old Saxon), p. 76, and on p. 101,
Ik blive hyr, so ji havven genågd.
And, Thaz sie inan Gote giuntwortlon, so is giscriban in Goles sunö,
= *sicut scriptum est in lege Domini*; Tat. Harm. Evang., 7. 2.
Some, *adj.*, peaceable, 459, 590, and 552. It occurs only in the phrase
'unjt and soms'. From A.S. som, some, *sb.*, = agreement, concord;
and this is most probably connected with *same*. Compare i-some.
Sonne, *sb.*, sun, as a noun fem., 101, 157. Compare *earth*, L 95, and
sea in Halliwell's text, p. 67.
Sore, *adv.*, grievously, 314.
Soþschape, *sb.*, truth, 1020.
Soul, *sb.*, plur. soulen, 448.
Spot, *sb.*, spittle, 1147. A.S. spatl, under which Bosworth gives Old
Germ. *spai*, Sw. *spott*.
Springe, *v.n.*, (of the heart), break, 593. Compare—
An Olymes hys herte nye *sprange*. Mort Arth. (Roxb. Cl.), p. 127.
Stat, *sb.*: broujt in stat = aided, 1206. Fr. secursz. Compare the German
idiom, einem zu Statten kommen, to assist any one.
Still, *adv.* The phrase *stille and loud* occurs twice in our poem, 994
and 1212. The more usual *loud and still* will be found in O. and
N., 1253, Handl. Synne, 1130, and Roxb. Cl. Morte Arthur, p. 7
(To be thy knight lowde and stille)
and p. 125. And in Rein. de Fos, p. 43, we read—
Ja, it sy *lüdbdr ofte stille*,
It ga mi darna wo it wille!
Streonynge, *sb.*, begetting, 1380.
Studefastschipe, *sb.*, established virtue, *constantia*, 282.
Sugge, *v.n.*, say, 420, 423, 438, &c. A.S. secgan. In the places quoted,
this verb rhymes with *jugge* = judge, and thus the pronunciation is
determined. That the Fr. *juge* was not sounded with a hard *g* is
clear from its etymology; and that the Fr. soft *g* was not in the
middle ages sounded as at present, but rather as we sound it, and
like the *gg* in Italian, is shown by the Greek form of *homægium*—

88   GLOSSARY.

itself only the Latin form of a French word—ὁμοίσιον (Montf. Pal. Gr., p. 434).

Sunderlyng, *adv.*, separately, 790.

Sunge, *v.n.*, sin, 1381.

Sunne-streon, *sb.*, begetting of sons, 1462.

Sunne, *sb.*, sin, 1140. We find both this form and *sone* in Wright's L. P., pp. 23, 24; 'In sunne ant sorewe', and '*Sone* is solel'.

Suwe, *v.a.*, follow, 1274.

Swipe, *adv.*, exceedingly, 1039. Compare the Friesic 'te *suithe*' = nimis, Rechtsqn., p. 12.

Take, *v.a.*, give, surrender, 202.

Tell, *v.n.*, attach value, give heed, 981.

Teon, *v.a.*, draw: hence, as a *v.n.*, to go, 821, 877. For this transition of meaning compare the Germ. *ziehen* as used reflexively. But the Old Saxon form of *ziehen*, *tên*, is used exactly as in our text; e. g.

 Frouwe Ermelyn sprak altohand:
 Shole wi nu *tên* in ein ander land,
 Dâr wi âlende unde fromde weren? R. de Fox, p. 100.

Tyme, *sb.*, hour, 1403. Compare the use of *tyme* as = month in—
 After was it monthes two
 As frely folke it vndyr stode,
 Or our gawayne myght ryde or go,
 Or had fote vpon erthe to stonde.
 The ilj *tyme* he was full thro,
 To do batayle w^t herte and hande.
     Morte Arthur (Roxb. Cl.), p. 96.

Tipelynge, *sb.*, tithe, tenth part, 1180.

To, *prep.*, omitted before the infinitive mood when another *to* follows, 976 (where see note), 990, 1163, 1524. Other examples are—
 Marie wente away;
 þe monek rod nijt and day
 Folke to gode bringe
 Dore þis like pinge, &c.

i. e. 'folke to gode *to* bringe', (MS. Bodl. Digby 86, fol. 132). So in Chaucer's Monkes Tale, De Alexandro Magno,
 They were glad for pees unto him sende,
i. e. 'unto him *to* sende'. And in Handlyng Synne, L 1211,
 Þou art yn weye to peyne be broghte.

To, *prep.*, = for, as, 183, 506, 1091, 1424. Compare—
 Tac the rode *to* thy staf, Wright's L. P., p. 106.

To-bere, *v.a.*, bear different ways, separate, 522; part. *to-boren*, = at enmity, 49. Compare Gr. διαφέρεσθαι, to be at variance.

To-dreynen, *v.a.*, prove, 974. A curious instance of the A. S. prefix *to* with a French verb.

GLOSSARY. 89

Tokening, *sb.*, meaning, thing signified, 557.
To-tle, *v. n.*, lie in an opposite direction, 1000.
Torne, *v. a.*, turn: tornen out, 1211, = turn round, change. Fr. has—
    Ta fol ne peut rien *changer*.
Tour, *sb.*, turn, 1334, where see note.
To-yeynes, *prep.*, against, 366, 1097. A.S. to-gegnes. The same word is also used in Lay. Br., Ancren Riwle, &c.; and apparently as an *adverb* in Rel. S., l. 18, which I venture to read and render thus:
    Ne mai no mon þar *to-yeines*,
 nor may any man endure (that = tharne)—or, be bold (thar = dare, θαρρειν)—against him.
Treatise, *sb.*, in the Introductory lines: date probably not later than 1370.
Truth, *sb.*, belief, 1207. Fr.—
    Nostre *creance* o nostre fol.

Þat, as a compound *relative*, = *he that*, or in the language of the nineteenth century, *he who*, 1. I do not remember to have met with another instance of the pronoun so used. There is an approach to this use in 1489, 1490, but there the *he* is expressed in the latter part of the line.—Þat = him þat = to him who, 708.
Þat, *rel. pron.*, supported by the personal pron., as in Modern German, Ich *der ich* ihn kenne; 360, 1046, 1129, 1283, 1322. In A.S. the pers. pron. preceded, as, Ic som Gabriel ic þe stande beforan Gode. With the passage in our poem compare Fragm. on the Seven Sins, st. 17,
    Þat þou art in hit so proute. ne sal þe leue neuer a cloute,
that is apparently—unless þat here = though—'never a rag shall remain to thee *who* art so proud of it' (thy fine raiment). Yet clearer is the line in Sir Amadace, 53. 5,
    I hane a doȝtur, *that* my nayre *ho* isse.
Compare Handl. Synne, l. 4122, and Moral Ode, st. 147,
    Þer buð þo hepenemen. þe were lawe lass
    Þe heom nas nout of godes bede. ne of godes hesse;
i. e. *quibus* fult nihil &c. And compare the common vulgarism of *which* thus followed by a personal pronoun: 'Inspector Deedles, *wich he* mite be called Needles, said to me Distink &c.' Punch, Dec. 19, 1863.
Þat = where?, l. 56. In the text of this passage I have allowed þat to stand, and regret it. I have no doubt þer is the true reading: compare ll. 666 and 748. Þat is sometimes = *when* (as in Luke 19. 43), but never = *where;* for we do sometimes mark time when by a noun without a preposition (as 'I saw him last Monday'), but never place where.
[Þat, *rel. pr.*, redundant after *what*, 287. It is necessary to justify by examples the emendation on which I have ventured. This use of þat is familiar enough in the phrases *who that, which that, whosoever that*

(which occurs as late even as Lily's Euphues), *whether that, while that, as that, when this, though that, why that, how that, lest that, wherefore that, if that, where that*, &c., all of which, and several other such, occur frequently in Chaucer, and see ll. 44, 109, 272, 442, in our poem. But it is sufficient to exemplify *what that*, thus. We have (1.) the two words separated, and used as a dependent interrogative, in

I recche naught *what* wrong *that* thou me profre,
Seconnde Nonnes Tale, and in the Prologue,
And eek in *what* array *that* they were inne.

(2.) The words separated, and used as a relative, in '*What* man *that* is norisshed by Fortune, sche maketh him a gret fool,' Tale of Melibæus; and in the Prologe of the Chanounes Yeman,
What maner man *that* causeth him therto.

And so in Handlyng Synne, l. 4346.

(3.) The words together, used in a dependent question, in the same Prologe,
What schulde I telle .....
And of moche other thing *what that* ther was?

and again (ibid.)
And in myn herte wondren I bigan
What that he was, &c.

(4.) As in our poem, the words together, and used as a relative,—
But *what that* God forwot moot needes be,

The Nonne Prest his Tale; and in the Tale of Melibæus, 'Every man crieth and clatereth *what that* him liketh.' Many more examples might easily be adduced.]

Þat, *art.*, the, 139, 169, 170, &c.

Þat, *conj.*, = so that, 638, 1250, as commonly in Old English. Compare—
Hinse begunde to ropen do
Wemodigen mid enem drovigen gelate
Dat Reinke dat hörde buten dem gate, R. de F., p. 37.

Þat, *conj.*: that ne = Lat. *quin*, 6.

Þat, *conj.*, = quin, quominus, 220, 430. Compare Handl. Synne, l. 3546.

Þat, *conj.*, noûll, 1412. So *the tone* = that one = *until* one, in the following;
Be-segitte we ware;
On a day we venbet oute,
And toke presonerus stonte,
The tone of owre foloys had doute,
And durst nolte faribe face. Avowynge of Arther, 64.

And in Ancren Riwle, p. 64,—auh we schulen leten smecchunge vort tet we spoken of ower mete. So in French que often = jusqu'à ce que, as, Attendes qu'il vienne.

Þat, *conj.*, = though, (or *though that*, Chaucer's usual form), 20, and perhaps 360. Compare the words of Satanas in the Harrowing of Hell

(MS. Bodl. Digby 86, fol. 119),
    Ihu welcomen þou be
    þal falsore rewaþ me
    þou art lonerd oner al
    þou bauest þat þou habbe shal
    Heuene and erþe weldest þou þe
    þe sonles in helle let þou be
    þat Ich haue let me holde
    þat þou bauest wel mote þou welde.
So *que* is used for *bien que* or *quoique* in French; and so in Latin *quod* is at times almost = *quamvis*, as in Ter. Eun. 5. 8. 34, where see Parry's note for other examples.

Þauh, *conj.*, yet, 1296, 1504. Þauh is often so used in Ancren Riwle; for example,—mi cume and mi wunlunge, þauh bit þuoche altri, hit is þauh heslawinds, p. 190. Compare *3it*.

Þenke, þenche, *v. a.*, think, 1, 17. A.S. þencan.

Þer, *adv.*, used redundantly with verbs, as in *there is* = il y a, 491, 504 (A.), 736, 740 (V.). So in Friesic, Jef *ther* inene brothere send, if there be two brothers, Hechtsqu., p. 52, b.

Þer-mide, *adv.*, therewith, associated in it, 374.

Þewe, *sb.*, servant, 763.

Þewdome, þewedam, *sb.*, bondage, 347, 434.

Þing, *sb.*, of the same form in the plur.; 5, 8, &c. On þinge see note on 830, and compare 842.

Þolemodnesse, *sb.*, patience, 985.

Þolyen, *v. a.*, suffer, 410. A.S. polian.

Þon, *dem. pron.*, acc. of þat: bi þon = by this, by that, 1196, 1261.

Þrillihed, *sb.*, trinity, 9, 1239, 1503, &c. From A S. *þrilic* = of three, third, LaL trinus; and the abstract noun termination -*hád* or -*hod*. Ormin uses *þrimnnesse*. The A.S. forms are *þrines*, *þrinis*, &c.

Þrow, *v. a.*, to make circular, 739. The A.S. prawan, and the cognate Latin torqueo, both primarily signify circular motion.

Þurle, *v. a.*, pierce, 1152. A.S. þirlian.

Uchone = each one, followed by a redundant *he*, 1228.
Underfonge, *v. a.*, receive, undergo, 661. A.S. underfón. Fr. has recevoir.
Undernime, *v. a.*, relieve, deliver, 1420.
Understand, *v. a.*, serve, obey, 140, 246, 254, 933, and 1045. The sense approaches this also in 395, 426, 566, and 1074, where it is rather, listen, pay attention, as in Moral Ode 115,
    Vnder-stondet nu to me. reidj men & earme
    Ic wulle telle of belle pine. & warnie ow wiđ berme—
i. e. '*Listen* now to me: &c.'—In other passages in our poem this verb bears its common meaning, as perhaps in 1231. In 1131 it is used reflexively.

Unmete, *adj.*, unmeasured, abnormal, monstrous, 634. A.S. unmete.
Unworþ, *adj.*, worthless, 1112.
Unwreste, *sb.*, sin, 335.
Unwreste, *adj.*, base, wicked, 1149.
Unwrestliche, *adv.*, wickedly, 1468.
Unwrestschupe, *sb.*, wickedness, 1143.
Up-brake, *v.n.*, to burst out (with some speech), to exclaim, 437. And compare O. and N., 200. In German, Dutch, and Danish, are similar compounds, but not in precisely this sense.
Upnime, *v.a.*, take up: pret., upnom, 1468.

Weed, *sb.*, garment, pl. *weden*, 547. Tat. has *giuuati* (= provincial Germ. *gewate*) = vestimentum, c. 13, 11. In 667 *werd* = body, as the garment of the soul.
West, *adj.*, wet, 1433. Besides the form *wete*, the A.S. wæt and the wæte of Orm both attest the long vowel in this word.
What, *int. adv.*, why, like *quid* and *tí*, 1061. So Wiclif writes, 'Whæt seken ȝe hym?' Luke 24. 5. Reineke de Fos, p. 8,
Wat wôrde shôlen dâr mêr av wâsen?
= why should there be more words about it? And in Tat., 'Was toufist thu thanne?' = *quid* ergo baptizas? And, 'Wib uuas nuofis?' = woman, why weepest thou?
Wher, *interr. adv.*, contracted form of *whether*, 1040. We now use *whether* (and *where* as a dialectic variety) only in dependent sentences. In our text it asks a direct question, as in Wiclif's version of Luke 24. 26, and in The Cokes Tale of Gamelyn:
'Adam,' seyde Gamelyn, 'what is now thy reed?
Wher I go to my brother and girde of his heed?'
So in the Morte Arth. (Roxb. Cl), p. 17,
'Ector,' he sayd, '*where* thon it were
That wonndid me thns woundir sore?'
This form occurs in Anglo-Saxon (Rask's Gram., p. 60) and Laȝ., and not merely 'kept its ground in Middle English till the fifteenth century,' as Sir Frederick Madden states (Laȝ. Br., Gloss. Rem., p. 466), but occurs at least as late as Shakspere,—
Good sir, say *wher* yon 'll answer me or no,
Comedy of Errors, 4. 1; and Ben Jonson,
Who shall doubt, Donne, *wher* I a poet be?
Epigram 96. And in the western dialects it still survives, but only, as in Shakspere, as a dependent interrogative, and also with *or = sive* ... *sive*, as in Mrs. Gwatkin's Devonshire Dialogue: 'I told en, *ware* a know'd it or no, my Dame was above doing ort in a hugger-mugger manner.' As to the form, compare *wer* contracted from *weder* in Reineke de Fos: e. g.
He konde nigt gân, *wer* nu edder fér,

GLOSSARY. 93

i. e. 'He could not go, neither near nor far,' where wer ... adder almost = sive ... sive.
Which, adj., = qualis, 53.
Which, adj., = quantus, 110.
Who, interr.pron., 268; and see Ho. I have pointed out elsewhere (Trans. 1860-1, pp. 64 sqq.) that in early English who in the nom. case is used only (1.) as an interrogative, as in our poem, (2.) much more rarely as a relative under the same restrictions as the German wer. Such, it appears to me, is its use in the passage quoted (Tr. 1860-1, p. 299) by the Rev. J. Eastwood, where the who is not the simple relative but = the he that of the Auth. Vers., in other words = wer. In the next quotation (Ib., p. 300) it is quite a mistake to call wo a relative; it is a dependent interrogative. 'But wo is þe formar .... I drede ongly to say', i. e. 'Quis autem effector sit .... dicere reformido.' Also I would observe that who can hardly be said to have 'established itself as a relative', until it is used as such with all the facility of the Latin qui, as at present. The Siedge of Breda (1627) remains the earliest work in which I have found it so employed, and that work is the production of an Irishman.
[Who,] whom, rel.pron., used of things, 296, 857, 915, 1086, 1205. Compare Shakspere's
  If aught possess thee from me, it is dross,
  Usurping ivy, briar, or idle moss,
  Who, all for want of pruning, with intrusion
  Infect thy sap, and live on thy confusion.
Comedy of Errors, 2. 2. And in Romeo and Juliet, who is used of Juliet's lips, and of Juliet's sighs.
Wiht, sb., anything, 638. A.S. wuht, wiht. For no wihs see Nouht.
Wisdom: comp. Wreccheddam.
Wyse, v.a., direct, guide, 297.
Wysenesse, sb., wisdom, 291.
Wit, sb.: the 'wittes fyre', see 138 and note.
Wite, v.a., observe, 1256.
Wiþ, prep., against, 701, 826.
Wiþoute, wiþouten, prep., without, 4, 11, &c. The existence of the latter of these forms, like the A.S. wiðutan, shows that the final e of wiþoute may be sounded if the metre requires it.
Wyter, adj., intelligent, 75. A.S. witol.
Wone, v.a., impair, 232.
Wone, and Woning, sb., 778 and foll., fault, defect, 'deficientia, inopia, absentia', (Lye). Though 'synne and wone al is on', l. 233, yet the former seems rather to be positive, the latter negative.
Wone, sb., joy, delight, 528. A S. wyn; Lat. Br., wunne, wonna. But Fr. has—
  De ton sen de ta vertui.

World, sb., in 26, 570, 743 is used without any article preceding, like a proper name, as sunne is used in Ancren Riwle, p. 58.
Worse, v.a.; part. i-worsed = impaired, blemished, Fr. blemie, 811.
Wrecchedbam, sb., wretchedness, 408. The termination -dam, which is commonly -dom in English, (as in A. Saxon, Old Saxon, Swedish, and Danish), and -thum in Germ., appears as -dam in the Northumbrian of Tat., = maidenhood, though the usual form in that dialect is -inom, as si noisinome = ad sapientiam.
Wray, wrayh, v.a., covered, veiled, 916. Fr., dont il couvrit sa delle. A.S. wreon, pret. wreah. Tatian's word for revelation is intrigannesse, with which compare the A.S. bewrigennes = concealment; but how comes bewray now to signify uncover?

Yat, sb., gate, door, 699. Fr. bas porte. But the original meaning of the word as simply = passage, from the verb go, is well seen in Rein. de Fox, pp. 35 foll., where it is simply a hole in a wall.

De pape hadde de negt dâr beforen
Enen fan sinen hanen forloren,
Wente [= for] Reineke én gat hadde broken
Dorg de wand, &c.

Yelp, sb., glory, 1364. A.S. gilp.
Yeme, v.a., save; part. i-jemed, Fr. sauner, 448.
Yif, conj., whether, num, 1074.
Yit, conj., yet: = though, 1473. Compare þauh.
Yond, prep., through, 1448. A.S. geond.
Yore, adv., long, 1339.

www.ingramcontent.com/pod-product-compliance
Lightning Source LLC
Chambersburg PA
CBHW032237080426
42735CB00008B/901